All too often those who want to follow Jesus lose their way because they do not grasp the next steps in their walk with him. They hear the Good News and desire to move forward yet they don't have the proper tools to continue on the journey. Peter Walker's *The Jesus Way* is an excellent resource for all such people.

What the church today needs most are resources for Christian discipleship. In my work I see many people come to faith in Christ but struggle to find materials that will help jump-start them in their journey – to my dismay these are few and far between. Peter's book is easy to understand, well presented, and thorough – without being overwhelming. It is truly an ideal handbook for those starting out on the Jesus way.

This is also a superb book to take on international mission. Many people in the 'two-thirds world' do not have Bibles but, when guided through *The Jesus Way*, they can access the teaching of the New Testament in just twelve easy steps.

Peter Walker provides a clear and thoughtful model for following Jesus. He has done this with the insight of a biblical scholar and the enthusiasm of a passionate believer. He shows how following Jesus is a life filled with joy, triumph in trials, peace, love, and above all, hope. *The Jesus Way* provides us with a roadmap that leads to a deeper relationship with Jesus and an experience of his abundant life.

Carrie Boren
Missioner for Evangelism
Episcopal Diocese of Dallas

The Jesus Way

The Essential Christian Starter Kit

Peter Walker

MONARCH
BOOKS

Oxford, UK and Grand Rapids, Michigan, USA

First published in the UK in 2009 by Monarch Books
(a publishing imprint of Lion Hudson plc),
Wilkinson House, Jordan Hill Road, Oxford OX2 8DR.
Tel: +44 (0)1865 302750 Fax: +44 (0)1865 302757
Email: monarch@lionhudson.com
www.lionhudson.com

ISBN: 978-1-85424-908-1 (UK)
ISBN: 978-0-8254-6311-2 (USA)

Distributed by:
UK: Marston Book Services Ltd, PO Box 269, Abingdon, Oxon OX14 4YN;
USA: Kregel Publications, PO Box 2607, Grand Rapids, Michigan 49501

British Library Cataloguing Data
A catalogue record for this book is available from the British Library.

Printed and bound in Malta by Gutenberg Press.

For Archdeacon John Omagor
and the Christian leaders in the diocese of Kumi, Uganda
together with the members of 'Jim's A-team' in March 2004
You refreshed my heart in Christ.

PHILEMON 1:20

Contents

Acknowledgements

I am extremely grateful to all those who have read this book in its (many!) draft stages through the last four years. These include friends from Christ Church, Abingdon (Karen, Brian, Judy, Andrew and Tim); those who taught this material in Uganda in August 2005 (Tom, Fiona, Richard and Steve and the other Tom); people associated with Wycliffe Hall or the Oxford Centre for Apologetics (Michael Green, Chris Boyce, Krish Kandiah, David Ingall, John Allister and Carrie Boren); and other wise guides such as Sam Allberry (formerly at St Ebbes' Oxford), Rico Tice (All Soul's Langham Place) and Graham Tomlin (now Dean of St Mellitus' College in the diocese of London). Thanks also to Tony Collins and Simon Cox at Monarch Book for their vision for this project.

I am grateful to Wycliffe for a period of study leave in 2004 when much of the book was first drafted; also to the parish of Grace Church in Colorado Springs who experienced an Easter sermon which unpacked chapters 1 to 4 at rather too great a length! Those who know the field of New Testament studies will be able to detect the influence of certain key people on my thinking (though any errors in my presentation of the New Testament must remain my own). These include my former, much-valued colleague, David Wenham, with his seminal sermons on Acts 1 – 5 (back in 1988!), and Tom Wright, Bishop of Durham, with his books and lectures on Jesus' kingdom agenda, the resurrection and Luke 24.

Three Easter Mondays stand out in my mind, as days when the importance of Luke 24 was impressed upon me: for the first two I was in the Holy Land (one, on my own, spent walking along the road to Emmaus in 1984; the other, with Tom Wright and our large tour party, celebrating communion near ancient Emmaus in 1998); but the third (strangely) was in northern Spain in 2004, delayed for several hours in the coffee lounge at Bilbao railway station. That's where the six 'building-blocks' first came into view. Such is life!

Peter Walker
Associate Vice-Principal and Tutor in New Testament
Wycliffe Hall, University of Oxford
November 2008

Foreword

The older I get, the more aware I become of the vital need to give new converts to Jesus Christ a top quality grounding in the realities of discipleship. Granted, Christ's love and faithfulness are such that he constantly keeps safe innumerable converts who are existing in what seems a permanent baby stage – Christians who were never properly discipled and who spiritually have never grown up. (*Thank you, Lord Jesus, for this further demonstration of your unfathomable love.*) But our Lord's ideal, as apostolically voiced, is of steady spiritual growth through solid grounding in divine things.

Young Christians, along with veteran Christians and all Christians in between, are called to 'walk' in Christ (the image is of sustained advance) 'rooted and built up in him and established in the faith ... abounding in thanksgiving' (Col 2:6–7). This is the unchanging agenda for the high-grade spiritual education necessary for discipling both the church's children (young people, that is, growing up in Christian homes) and first-generation believers, as the Colossians were.

We live in an age in which technology is making materialists out of the entire human race: countries with a Christian heritage become secular, multi-faith communities; and Christian homes, at least in the West, are crumbling. As a result, the discipling task has become a great deal more demanding than it once was. Yet in this same age God is bringing to birth a huge crop of converts worldwide, which makes the discipling task enormously urgent at the present time.

To be done well, every teaching task requires a focused intention and strong devotion on the part of teachers, plus high quality resources to draw on. Thus in the second century, when the church seriously tackled the task of winning the Roman Empire, catechetical classes for both casual enquirers and persons convinced about Christ who wanted to join the church were regularly maintained; and thoughtful writings of an apologetic-evangelistic cast were regularly produced. Then, from the sixteenth to the nineteenth century, following a thousand years of comparative neglect, this type of ministry blossomed again, as abundance of catechisms and related books (both Protestant and Catholic) bear witness.

More recently, however, this kind of material has been thought to be over authoritative, inappropriately institutionalized, and hopelessly outmoded. So catechizing in all its forms has largely dropped out of church life. The result is that good discipling material is now thin on the ground, and a renewal of both a didactic focus and catechetical resources has become urgent.

As in our time the world community has gone irreversibly global, so has the church. In saying this, I think particularly of mainstream evangelicalism which, through its many forms of denominational expression, I take to be the central and most authentic form of the Christian tradition, and which has certainly been at the heart of the extraordinary Christian expansion that has occurred since the second world war.

Clearly, this Christian globalization needs to be reflected in both the substance and the style of tomorrow's catechetical resources. And that is why I enthuse, as I do, about *The Jesus Way*. It seems to me the *most significant first step I have seen in this particular right direction*.

As little culture-specific and denomination-specific as it well could be, *The Jesus Way* brings out with ingenious thoroughness and appropriate fullness all the biblical basics of personal discipleship, and presents them in a thoroughly up-to-date, enlivening way. The fact that it was born cross-culturally, in and for Uganda, no doubt gave it a head start towards achieving the *world-Christian quality* that seems to me to mark it out.

May it herald the era of a catechetical renewal that I, along with others, long to see.

J.I. Packer
Vancouver, Canada
Easter, 2009

Introduction

Follow Jesus – *his* way

Jesus Christ is worth following – worth living your life for. To use one of his own images, he is truly the 'unusually fine pearl': A man is looking for fine pearls, and when he finds one that is unusually fine, he goes and sells everything he has, and buys that pearl. (See Matthew 13:45–46).

However, many people set out to follow Jesus but then, sadly, get lost. Sometimes this may be of their own choosing. Perhaps, deep down, they *wanted* to do their own thing (using Jesus as a convenient cover) and were not very interested in actually *following* Jesus. They would rather follow their own agendas.

Yet, others genuinely get confused. In many instances, the reason for this confusion boils down to this: they do not think of Jesus as a living Person who is able to give clear instructions about how to follow him – and who does so through the pages of the New Testament. Instead this ancient text, written by his first followers, remains something of a mysterious 'closed book' – the preserve of scholars or students of history. It is rarely seen for what it is – a living book through which Jesus speaks his 'master's voice' into our lives. Jesus said:

"My sheep listen to my voice; I know them, and they follow me."

JOHN 10:27

But too often, the sheep get sidetracked and veer off the path – because they do not recognise that it is in the New Testament that they can *truly hear Jesus' voice*.

Following Jesus, you see, is not meant to be a journey which is spent groping in the dark. Jesus has left us some fairly clear instructions. Of course, there are aspects of the New Testament that are hard to understand, or open to a variety of interpretation, but these 'grey areas' rarely, if ever, affect the central core of the apostles' teaching. So it *is* possible to follow Jesus *his* way – that is, as Jesus intends, and working within the spacious frameworks which he has provided. What we have to do is listen out carefully for those instructions and guidelines – given both by Jesus himself in his own teaching and by those whom he appointed as his 'special messengers' (or apostles*). If you like, the 'Jesus Way' was always meant to be followed *Jesus'* way.

Jesus can teach us how to follow him. Put another way, Jesus himself can lead us into *his* truth. Some people have found this diagram helpful at this point.

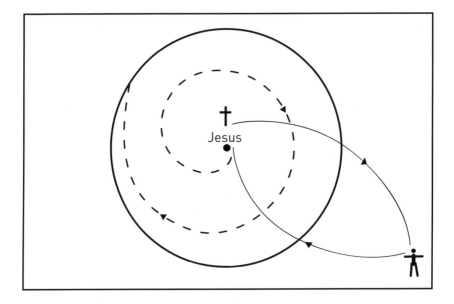

The circle represents all the truths of the Christian faith, spanning out from Jesus at the centre. Many people, when asked where they are on the diagram, place themselves outside the circle. They recognise they are not yet followers of Jesus. Some, however, would like to follow Jesus but they are a little hesitant: they are daunted by the circle (everything they don't know!) and, worse still, they don't know how to get inside the circle in the first place. The Good News is that the Risen Jesus, though he is at the centre of the circle, has the power to come outside the circle, to meet people exactly where they are, and then can take them *right back to the heart of the circle*. And from there it is *his* responsibility gradually to lead people outwards (in ever-increasing spirals!) into all the contents of the circle. So, if you would like to follow Jesus, or indeed have already begun to do so, you can have confidence that *he can lead you into all his truth*. Take hold of him, don't let him go, and he will then take full care of you. Let Jesus himself guide you along the Jesus Way.

How *The Jesus Way* was born

This book was born in the villages of Uganda. Invited in March 2004 to lead a team of Oxford students to meet Christian leaders in the remote area of Kumi (four hours north of Kampala), we also went out into the villages showing the *Jesus* film (reel to reel, generated from the back of a car, under the stars!). We found that so many people wanted to follow Jesus. But we were told by their pastors that Christian faith here often proves only skin-deep. There is a mammoth task of Christian education, training people in discipleship*. New followers of Jesus, they said, often just do not know how to continue – not helped by the lack of teaching resources and indeed of Bibles.

It was a humbling experience. Many of the pastors – those responsible for helping others to follow Jesus – themselves did not possess a copy of the Bible. So to see their joy, as we presented each of them with their own Bible, was moving indeed. And it made me acutely aware just how privileged I was to have been taught the New Testament from a young age by those who loved Jesus. Having taught the New Testament for several years to those training for ministry in the UK and USA, I now found myself in Uganda teaching this same precious book, and together we saw its majesty and beauty coming to light before our eyes. At that moment, I saw in a new way the great treasure on which I had been sitting. The New Testament – like Jesus himself (naturally!) – is a 'pearl' of great value, 'unusually fine'. It comes from him and reflects his brilliance. It's a book, therefore, that cannot be left in academic libraries, but must be enjoyed and then shared. It's a life-changing book. Indeed it's a living book, focused on Jesus who himself is a living person, and so it must be *lived out* in real lives.

So, looking out on the mud-huts from our jeep window as we said our farewells, I resolved to try and write a book that might introduce people to the truths of the New Testament *even if they never had a copy of it*. What, I wondered, if all that people knew of it was just two chapters? Which would they be? By the time we had reached Kampala, Luke 24 and Acts 2 had come clearly into view: two key chapters (covering the climax of Luke's gospel and the effective launch of Jesus' church), which I sensed could act as a brilliant, clear window into the whole of the rest of the New Testament.

The Jesus Way is the result: a book in two parts, learning first from Jesus himself and then from his apostles about what it means to follow Jesus – his way. To use the imagery of the circle, my prayer is that Jesus himself would take these pages and use them to lead his people into all of his truth.

Using this book

The Jesus Way is written for anyone who wants to follow Jesus. Some may feel they have not quite started yet, but, even so, would be interested to get an overview of the New Testament's teaching; quite rightly, before setting out on the journey, they want to know what they might be letting themselves in for! Such readers may find some of the material in the Appendices particularly useful, as they consider carefully the unique claims of Jesus and the arguments for his being raised from death. This may help them get clearer in their own mind why it's so important to set out on the Jesus Way.

Others know they have started out on the road, however falteringly. The twelve main chapters are written especially for you. As those who already aspire to be Jesus' followers today, we tune in to what Jesus taught his first followers and then to how those same followers taught others. So *The Jesus Way* is primarily intended to help 'nurture' and grow any such new believers. Here are twelve key topics that Jesus' modern-day followers need to grasp.

This book can be worked through by individuals on their own. There's quite a lot of material in each chapter, so it may be best to pace yourself – perhaps aiming for one chapter a week. You might even find it helpful to read it alongside someone else who has perhaps been trying to follow Jesus for a little longer and who can talk with you about the issues raised.

Alternatively, it could be used by study groups. In particular, local church leaders might like to use it for any 'follow-up' groups, perhaps for people who have been on courses like *Alpha* or *Christianity*

Explored. Those who have made a new or fresh commitment to Christ – whether on such courses or through other means – often need real guidance for those next, crucial months. *The Jesus Way* might be a real resource here. It could also be used by those preparing people for adult baptism* or confirmation*; in adult 'Sunday schools' (popular in North America) or at a church's 'weekend away', or as part of the church's training of its lay leaders*. Returning to Uganda in 2005, for example, we taught it as a course for lay ministers; those responsible for leading smaller, local churches.

All these, as J.I. Packer reminds us in his foreword, are forms of 'catechesis' – what the first Christians called basic instruction for new believers. In modern terms we might call it a 'starter kit' – either for new Christians or for those who want to go back and rediscover the essentials of their faith. Either way, it is a vital task and I pray that *The Jesus Way* might really help us at this critical point.

Special features of *The Jesus Way*

Several features of the book's design are worth noting. Because *The Jesus Way* is a pocket guide to the New Testament, it inevitably refers to the apostles' writings on almost every page. Many of these references are given only in verse references (e.g. Acts 19:20); some verses, however, are quoted in full in the main text. Some key sentences from the book have also been highlighted as 'Pop-up Quotes', designed to help you navigate your way more easily through the chapter. Each chapter also contains some 'boxed' material (often a summary of New Testament teaching on that chapter's subject).

The Jesus Way is deliberately designed for 'beginners', so I have tried to avoid complex jargon. Occasionally, however, it has been necessary to use a word that might require some further explanation for those unfamiliar with it. Such words are marked in the text by an asterisk after the word (e.g. apostles*). That further explanation can then be found in the glossary, together with a discussion of some related points of difficulty. The glossary is thus intended to help those who may want to pursue particular matters in more detail.

A look at the contents page will show how the book has been deliberately structured in two equal halves, each with six chapters.

Some may like to think of these as *key steps* along the JESUS WAY. Yet, after the first three (which probably must be the *first* three such steps), the order is not that important: in other words, it is not as though you cannot proceed to the next step until you have first mastered the previous one! This is not a regimented programme that has to be completed in strict order.

Instead, then, the language of 'building-blocks' has been used throughout: these are twelve key ingredients – twelve key bricks, if you like – which need to be in place if we are effectively to build a faithful Christian life. So (for reasons that become clear in the epilogue) I have developed the visual motif of an archway being constructed with six building-blocks on each side. If you find this helpful, that's great; but 'no worries', if not!

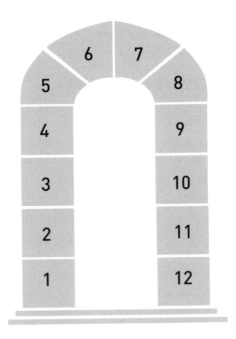

12 Key Building-blocks

– For Following Jesus Today

PART 1

Learning from Jesus Himself

(Luke 24)

From Luke's First Book:

His 'Good News' about Jesus (chapter 24)

The Resurrection (verses 1–12)

Very early on Sunday morning the women went to the tomb, carrying the spices they had prepared. They found the stone rolled away from the entrance to the tomb, so they went in; but they did not find the body of the Lord Jesus. They stood there puzzled about this, when suddenly two men in bright shining clothes stood by them. Full of fear, the women bowed down to the ground, as the men said to them, "Why are you looking among the dead for one who is alive? He is not here; he has been raised. Remember what he said to you while he was in Galilee: 'The Son of Man must be handed over to sinners, be crucified, and three days later rise to life'."

Then the women remembered his words, returned from the tomb, and told all these things to the eleven disciples and all the rest. The women were Mary Magdalene, Joanna, and Mary the mother of James; they and the other women with them told these things to the apostles. But the apostles thought that what the women said was nonsense, and they did not believe them. But Peter got up and ran to the tomb; he bent down and saw the linen wrappings but nothing else. Then he went back home amazed at what had happened.

The Walk to Emmaus (verses 13–35)

On that same day two of Jesus' followers were going to a village named Emmaus, about 11 kilometres from Jerusalem, and they were talking to each other about all the things that had happened. As they talked and discussed, Jesus himself drew near and walked along with them; they saw him, but somehow did not recognize him. Jesus said to them, "What are you talking abut to each other, as you walk along?"

They stood still, with sad faces. One of them, named Cleopas, asked him, "Are you the only visitor in Jerusalem who doesn't know the things that have been happening there these last few days?"

"What things?" he asked.

"The things that happened to Jesus of Nazareth," they answered. "This man was a prophet and was considered by God and by all the people to be powerful in everything he said and did. Our chief priests and rulers handed him over to be sentenced to death, and he was crucified. And we had hoped that he would be the one who was going to set Israel free! Besides all that, this is now the third day since it happened. Some of the women of our group surprised us; they went at dawn to the tomb, but could not find his body. They came back saying they had seen a vision of angels who told them that he is alive. Some of our group went to the tomb and found it exactly as the women had said, but they did not see him."

Then Jesus said to them, "How foolish you are, how slow you are to believe everything the prophets said! Was it not necessary for the Messiah to suffer these things and then to enter his glory?"

And Jesus explained to them what was said about himself in all the Scriptures, beginning with the books of Moses and the writings of all the prophets.

As they came near the village to which they were going, Jesus acted as if he were going farther; but they held him back, saying, "Stay with us; the day is almost over and it is getting dark." So he went in to stay with them. He sat down to eat with them, took the bread, and said the blessing; then he broke the bread and gave it to them. Then their eyes were opened and they recognized him, but he disappeared from their sight. They said to each other, "Wasn't it like a fire burning in us when he talked to us on the road and explained the Scriptures to us?"

They got up at once and went back to Jerusalem, where they found the eleven disciples gathered together with the others and saying, "The Lord is risen indeed! He has appeared to Simon!"

The two then explained to them what had happened on the road, and how they had recognized the Lord when he broke the bread.

Jesus Appears to his Disciples (verses 36–49)

While the two were telling them this, suddenly the Lord himself stood among them and said to them, "Peace be with you."

They were terrified, thinking that they were seeing a ghost. But he said to them, "Why are you alarmed? Why are these doubts coming up in your minds? Look at my hands and my feet, and see that it is I myself. Feel me, and you will know, for a ghost doesn't have flesh and bones, as you can see I have."

He said this and showed them his hands and his feet. They still could not believe, they were so full of joy and wonder; so he asked them, "Have you anything here to eat?" They gave him a piece of cooked fish, which he took and ate in their presence.

Then he said to them, "These are the very things I told you about while I was still with you; everything written about me in the Law of Moses, the writings of the prophets, and the Psalms had to come true."

Then he opened their minds to understand the Scriptures, and said to them, "This is what is written; the Messiah must suffer and must rise from death three days later, and in his name the message about repentance and the forgiveness of sins must be preached to all nations, beginning in Jerusalem. You are witnesses of these things. And I myself will send upon you what my Father has promised. But you must wait in the city until the power from above comes down upon you."

Jesus is Taken Up to Heaven (verses 50–53)

Then he led them out of the city as far as Bethany, where he raised his hands and blessed them. As he was blessing them, he departed from them and was taken up into heaven. They worshipped him and went back into Jerusalem, filled with great joy, and spent all their time in the Temple giving thanks to God.

1

Enjoy Jesus' Resurrection

"Why are you looking among the dead for one who is alive? He is not here; he has been raised."

LUKE 24:5–6

Resurrection at the centre

Was Jesus really raised from the dead? Luke, the writer of this key chapter in the Bible, was in no doubt. It might seem bizarre and without any parallel, but yes, three days after his public execution in Jerusalem*, Jesus, so Luke claims, was seen by his followers.

First, he writes, Jesus' tomb was found to be empty; next, Jesus met a couple of his followers making their way to a village outside Jerusalem called Emmaus*; and finally, back in Jerusalem later that first Easter* day, he met with his followers – showing them his wounds, and eating some food to prove he was no ghost. At the start of the day, his followers had thought the first rumours were a load of 'nonsense'; but by the day's end, sheer 'joy' and exhilaration was evidently beginning to pulse through their lives (Luke 24:11, 41).

This resurrection* of Jesus has, ever since, been the central claim of authentic Christian faith – that the living God raised Jesus Christ bodily from the grave. And the news that Jesus is alive continues to this day to turn people's expectations upside down, bringing joy and new hope. This can be true for anyone – it can be true for you. Those who meet with this Risen Jesus are a given a whole new life; and those who are serious about following him are in for a life characterised by adventure and new possibilities.

Jesus wants this truth about his resurrection to become the very centre of your thinking and your life. He made that clear to his first followers on that first Easter day; but he has been doing it ever since. Jesus is truly back from the dead – he is alive!

Following a living Jesus

The resurrection has always been at the heart of the Christian message. After all, take the resurrection away and what are you left with?

- A teacher who dies in his 30s as a failed Messiah*.
- Someone who makes great promises about God but who comes to a pitiful end.
- An example of a good, truthful person being hounded to death by human evil at its worst.

Not much good news here! No wonder there are so few people who try to 'follow' Jesus whilst denying his resurrection. No wonder, if they do, that their teaching has such little impact. For why should we bother with a dead Jesus? Anything *nice* in his teaching (for example, about God's love) we probably want to believe already. On the other hand, anything *challenging* we can readily dismiss, since he's dead and gone. In that sense, we don't have to *follow* him at all — we're the ones who do the choosing. Above all, if Jesus remained dead in the tomb, his teaching and public ministry had evidently not been very successful; moreover, there is no clear reason for assuming that anything he said is necessarily true.

But put the resurrection back in its proper place — at the very centre — and things start to look quite different. Now, instead, we have

> It is love that truly stands at the heart of the universe.

a Jesus in whom God was evidently at work. It becomes vital to know what he said and what he did, for it all comes with the stamp of divine approval. Moreover, because of the resurrection, Jesus' words and actions have the power to bring God's truth and love dramatically into our lives today.

Then again, with the resurrection at the centre, hope for the future has a solid foundation: in particular, physical death need not be the end, and our present lives can be seen as infinitely valuable. We find we are living in a God-invaded world, with God himself able to become our greatest reality. Indeed we can sense how it is love that truly stands at the heart of the universe.

In addition, we are given a clear vision of God's purpose, not only for our own lives, but for the whole world: we are to live out Jesus' teaching, to implement his kingdom, to proclaim his rule, and to work 'hand in hand' with the God who has the power to bring good out of evil, and light out of darkness. The true and living God is the God of resurrection power, the one who is at work to restore his broken world. We too, then, are to be an 'Easter people', bringing the resurrection light of Jesus into our local worlds – into God's world.

So, no resurrection – no Good News. No resurrection – no 'Christianity' worth its name. If there's no resurrection, then there's no point in following Jesus. Indeed there's no point in walking in the Jesus Way or reading any more of this book. For we are looking together in these pages at what it means to follow a living person – not a dead one. Jesus, according to the New Testament writers, is alive – and that means alive *today*!

So the first 'building block' as we seek to follow this Jesus – the first step along the Jesus Way – is to *enjoy Jesus' resurrection* and to enjoy living each day of our lives in the light of this amazing reality. If, right now, you do not feel so sure about the truth of the resurrection, or if you want to invest some time looking in more detail at the historical evidence for it, then you may find it helpful to turn now to Appendix B (The Resurrection of Jesus: Can We Be Sure?), to look at the various objections to the resurrection and begin to develop your own response. It's good to build up one's confidence on this vital, life-changing topic.

In the rest of this chapter, however, we will move on to consider the implications of all this. What does the New Testament teach us about the meaning and significance of the resurrection (see Box 1)? If the resurrection of Jesus really happened, what difference will it make? We will find it will give us a whole new vision of who God is, but also of what he wants us to do in response.

Box 1 – Resurrection in the New Testament: some selected texts

Jesus said to [Martha], "I am the resurrection and the life. Those who believe in me will live, even though they die. ... Do you believe this?"
JOHN 11:25–26

[Jesus] said to Thomas, "Put your finger here, and look at my hands; then stretch out your hand and put it in my side. Stop your doubting, and believe!"
Thomas answered him, "My Lord and my God!"
JOHN 20:27–28

For 40 days after his death he appeared to them many times in ways that proved beyond doubt that he was alive. They saw him, and he talked with them about the Kingdom of God.

ACTS 1:3

But God raised him from death three days later and caused him to appear, not to everyone, but only to the witnesses that God had already chosen, that is, to us who ate and drank with him after he rose from death. And he commanded us to preach the gospel to the people and to testify that he is the one whom God has appointed judge of the living and the dead.

ACTS 10:40–42 (PETER'S WORDS IN CAESAREA;
SEE ALSO, PAUL'S WORDS: ACTS 13:30–31; 17:30–31 AND 26:8)

The Good News ... about his Son, our Lord Jesus Christ: ... as to his divine holiness, he was shown with great power to be the Son of God by being raised from death. ... Christ was raised from death by the glorious power of the Father. ... For we know that Christ has been raised from death and will never die again – death will no longer rule over him.

ROMANS 1:2–3; 6:4, 9

He has ended the power of death and through the gospel has revealed immortal life. ... Remember Jesus Christ who was raised from death.

2 TIMOTHY 1:10; 2:8

"Don't be afraid! I am the first and the last. I am the living one! I was dead, but now I am alive for ever and ever."

REVELATION 1:17–18 (JESUS' WORDS IN JOHN'S VISION)

The God who raised Jesus

First, the resurrection teaches us four powerful truths about God himself – the God who raised Jesus.

1. The resurrection is strong evidence for God's existence

Debates about God's existence continue unabated. Some, focusing on issues of creation* or evolution*, argue that science has disproved the 'God theory'. Others, looking at evil and suffering in the world, see no evident place for a God of power and love. Yet the resurrection of Jesus cuts into this debate with clarity, bringing something new to the table. For, if we look here – at the resurrection – we will find fresh evidence, surprisingly clear, of the activity of the God of power and love.

So, for many, the resurrection is the clearest sign that God truly exists and is able to work in his world, and that we do not live in a closed, 'God-less' universe. Thus the New Testament writers (as seen in Box 1) frequently refer to the resurrection as an act of *God*: it was not so much that Jesus rose (by his *own* will), but rather that *God raised Jesus* from death: 'God raised him from death' (Acts 2:24; 10:40; 13:30); 'God has raised from death our Lord Jesus' (Hebrews 13:20). They also see the resurrection as demonstrating God's great *power*:

> *This power working in us is the same as the mighty strength which he used when he raised Christ from death.*
>
> EPHESIANS 1:19–20

2. The resurrection introduces us to God's holiness

For the apostle Paul, the resurrection reveals the 'divine holiness' of Jesus (see his words in Romans 1:3 in Box 1). It also reveals the holiness of God. This involves two aspects – both his love and his judgement. Speaking to the Athenians about the resurrection, Paul brought out this solemn theme of judgement:

> *He will judge the whole world with justice by means of a man he has chosen. He has given proof of this to everyone by raising that man from death!*
>
> ACTS 17:31

In the resurrection, God was declaring his vindication of Jesus and of all who would then come to him. He was also thereby appointing him to be the final judge of 'everyone' throughout 'the whole world'. The resurrection is a signal that God will judge the world by his holiness at the end of time – and he will do this through Jesus.

3. The resurrection reveals God's love

In the resurrection, we see God coming back to all people with a message of forgiveness. Human beings may do their worst against God – hating him, even crucifying him – but they have an opportunity to be forgiven and restored. Peter, though he had denied Jesus three times, was given, through the resurrection, a second chance (Mark 14:66–72; John 21:15–19). So the God who has set a future day for judgement has also made this present time an opportunity to return to him – what the Bible calls a 'day to be saved*' (Acts 4:12; Romans 13:11; 2 Corinthians 6:2). He is indeed a holy God but, deep within that, he is truly a God of compassion and grace, of forgiveness and love.

4. The resurrection reveals God's purposes

The New Testament writers saw the resurrection as being the crowning fulfilment of God's purposes as already revealed in the Old Testament, by which God was now bringing the world into a new age, the age of fulfilment (1 Corinthians 10:11). Yet the resurrection also signals his purposes for the future: God is intending to bring in a 'new creation', not abandoning our physical world but transforming it through his resurrection power (see further below chapter 12).

The Jesus who was raised

The resurrection also teaches us a vast amount about Jesus himself. Note what the New Testament writers say about Jesus in the light of his resurrection:

- He is the person appointed to be the 'judge of the living and the dead' (Acts 10:42; see also Acts 17:31, quoted just above).
- He is the 'Great Shepherd of the sheep', who calls us to belong in his fold (Hebrews 13:20).
- He is the 'Son of God', God's 'dear Son', whom we must 'listen to' and obey (Romans 1:4; see also Mark 9:7).
- He is the long-awaited 'Messiah' (or 'Christ') of Israel and is now the world's true ruler and king: "this Jesus ... is the one that God has made Lord and Messiah!"; "there is another king, whose name is Jesus" (Acts 2:36; 17:7).
- He is the 'Lord'. The first Christians expressed the heart of their faith in just three words: "Jesus is Lord!" (1 Corinthians 12:3). First-

century Jews used this title 'Lord' to describe the one true God of Israel; but now Jesus' followers were applying it to this human being, recently executed in Jerusalem, called Jesus.

The whole New Testament is littered with such references to Jesus as Messiah*, as the Son of God* and as the Lord*:

> He was shown with great power to be the Son of God by being raised from death.

ROMANS 1:4

Indeed, there are one or two places where it clearly hints that Jesus can be equated fully *with God himself* (see e.g. John 1:1–14 and fuller discussion below in chapters 9 and 12). So, even if Thomas' outburst on seeing the Risen Jesus was spontaneous and not fully thought through, it was profoundly true: "My Lord and my God!" (John 20:28).

The resurrection therefore reveals and establishes the unique identity of Jesus. Yes, other aspects of Jesus' life support this claim (the circumstances of his birth, his authoritative teaching, his powerful miracles, his sinless life), but the resurrection is like the capstone in the arch. Without the resurrection, the New Testament writers would never have dared to speak in such terms. With it, they could scarcely hold themselves back!

This Jesus is unique. Though clearly human, he must also be identified with God in some way. He is the king and the judge. He is also an eternal being. As one New Testament writer said:

> Jesus Christ is the same yesterday, today, and for ever!

HEBREWS 13:8

Meeting the Risen Jesus

If this is true, the consequences for all of us are important. The resurrection tells us that:

- we live in a world visited by God;
- God is interested in his created world and in all aspects of human life (including our physical bodies);

- there is a future for all of us after death (see chapter 12);
- the most important person — in this life and in the next — is Jesus himself.

Jesus is the centre of God's world and he must be the centre of our world too.

The resurrection thus presents everyone with a startling truth: Jesus is the true Lord of the world and we must meet him. He is God's appointed king and we must humble ourselves before him and, only so, enter into his kingdom. In the resurrection, God 'gave him the name that is greater than any other name. And so, in honour of the name of Jesus ... all will openly proclaim that Jesus Christ is Lord' (Philippians 2:9–11). God wants everyone to acknowledge the lordship of Jesus, his Risen Son. So Paul can write with great clarity:

> If you confess that Jesus is Lord and believe that God raised
> him from death, you will be saved.
>
> ROMANS 10:9

So, before going any further along the Jesus Way, we have to pause and perform a vital double-check. For, if recognising Jesus as the Risen Lord is the essential starting-point of the journey, are we sure that we have truly got started? We have to ask ourselves some life-changing questions:

- Have we truly responded to this challenge of Jesus as Lord?
- Are we quite clear that Jesus is risen from the dead and therefore alive today?

There is no point in reading further through this book if we know we have not responded in this way — or indeed, if we are slightly uncertain at this point. As they say in baseball, it is vital to 'get past first base'.

The Bible gives us a powerful picture to help us here. It is of the Lord Jesus Christ standing outside the door of everyone's house, wanting to come in: "Listen! I stand at the door and knock; if anyone hears my voice and opens the door, I will come in" (Revelation 3:20).

Many have found this picture helpful. They sense that Jesus has been outside their life, but unwelcomed — knocking on the door, but refused entry.

So the resurrection presents us, forcefully, with a Risen Jesus, to whom we must respond. We must 'open the door'. And the great news is that Jesus responds to any such opening of the door with those powerful words: "I will come in." This is a solemn promise, which is crystal clear and totally reliable.

Elsewhere, Jesus says: "I will never turn away anyone who comes to me" (John 6:37). The Risen Jesus never rejects anyone who sincerely turns to him. Some of us may feel very unimportant or quite unworthy; others may fear that, having perhaps experienced rejection by others, Jesus might do the same. Yet this promise of Jesus stands. It is for *anyone* who comes to him. Similarly, in Matthew's gospel, Jesus offers an identical invitation, matched by a firm promise: "Come to me, all of you who are tired from carrying heavy loads, and *I will give you rest*" (Matthew 11:28).

> The Risen Jesus never rejects anyone who sincerely turns to him.

The New Testament writers want us, then, to come to Jesus, to open the door of our lives to him, or – to use another of their pictures – to kneel before him as our rightful king, recognising that we ourselves are not truly in control of our lives (but Jesus *is*!).

People will respond to this challenge in many different ways. Our characters and circumstances are all unique, so there is no one formula. For some, the response is a gradual one, for others a quite sudden one. Yet at some point, we will need to verbalise some kind of response to the Risen Jesus – something which establishes communication between ourselves and him, something which recognises who he is and what he has done. In Paul's phrase, we will need to 'confess that Jesus is Lord'. The following words make up a simple prayer which is an example of what we might need to say to Jesus:

Lord Jesus, I now know you are the Lord and recognise you as my true king. You came from God; you died for me; you are alive today.

Please forgive me my sins; please forgive me for living my life without you.

I come to you; please receive me. I open the door and welcome you. Please now come into my life and stay with me, helping me to follow you day by day.

Amen

Some of us may wish to pause at this moment and re-echo that prayer in our own hearts; others know they have already prayed it at some point in the past. Either way, the good news is that the Risen Jesus always hears us when we pray such a prayer. We become his, and he becomes ours — for ever.

Living for him

If we have responded to the call of Jesus in some such way, then, from now on, our life is going to be bound up inevitably with this Risen Jesus. We will discover that being a Christian is not, primarily, obeying a set of commandments, but rather enjoying a relationship with a living person. Following in the Jesus Way is to follow a Jesus we already *know*!

In fact, we can now dare to think of Jesus as our 'friend'. Jesus said to his followers: "I call you friends" (John 15:15). This is an amazing privilege — to be friends with Jesus. Of course, this friendship will also involve the responsibility of obedience; note that Jesus also said:

> *You are my friends if you do what I command you.*
>
> JOHN 15:14

He is indeed our Lord whom we must obey, our king whom we must serve. Even so, he is also our friend and, as such, we should want to spend time in his company, getting to know him better. To be a Christian, writes Peter, is to be in love with Jesus:

> *You love him, although you have not seen him ...*
>
> 1 PETER 1:8

It is also, as Paul says, to *know* him:

> *All I want is to know Christ and to experience the power of his resurrection ...*
>
> PHILIPPIANS 3:10

Anyone who has responded to the Risen Jesus has embarked on exactly the same journey as Peter and Paul — an exciting journey of knowing and loving Jesus Christ better each day.

The rest of this book is designed to help you to grow in your relationship with Jesus. There will also be further explanation about how we too can share in Jesus' risen life – living our lives in the light of his resurrection power and promises (see chapters 10 and 12). For now, however, the first building-block needs to be firmly in place: it is to *enjoy Jesus' resurrection*.

If we are followers of Jesus, it is because he is alive and because he has called us to know him personally. We can enjoy his presence with us throughout our lives – and beyond.

Building-block 1

Enjoy Jesus' Resurrection – He is Alive!

2

Accept His Forgiveness

> *"The Messiah must suffer ... and in his name the message about repentance and forgiveness of sins must be preached ..."*
>
> LUKE 24:46–47

Luke 24, as a story, is all about the first Easter* day and resurrection*. Yet the Risen Jesus, in his own teaching here, focuses on something else – the meaning of his death. Jesus evidently wants us, as a matter of urgency, to understand why he died.

There is no doubting that Jesus truly died. The gospel writers describe the story of his last days in Jerusalem* and his crucifixion in great detail (see Luke 19 – 23). It is a gripping story, worth reading in detail. We see in it things repeated so much in our human history: betrayal, plotting, secret agreements, dashed hopes, unfair trials, human brutality, and heavy-handed tactics from those abusing their power. But it's a story that poses a much deeper question: 'Why?'

For there is equally no doubting that Jesus could easily have escaped – there was an empty desert under three miles away! Jesus deliberately went up to Jerusalem, performed some acts in the Temple which sorely provoked its leaders, and then hung around waiting to be arrested. What made him do it? What could he possibly achieve by giving himself up to such a cruel death?

Jesus teaches about his death – *after* the event

After the resurrection, this question would press upon his followers with great urgency: why had this person with evident authority *over* death placed himself *under* it?

The Risen Jesus begins to answer this question in Luke 24. In line with Old Testament teaching and prophecy, he asserts, it was

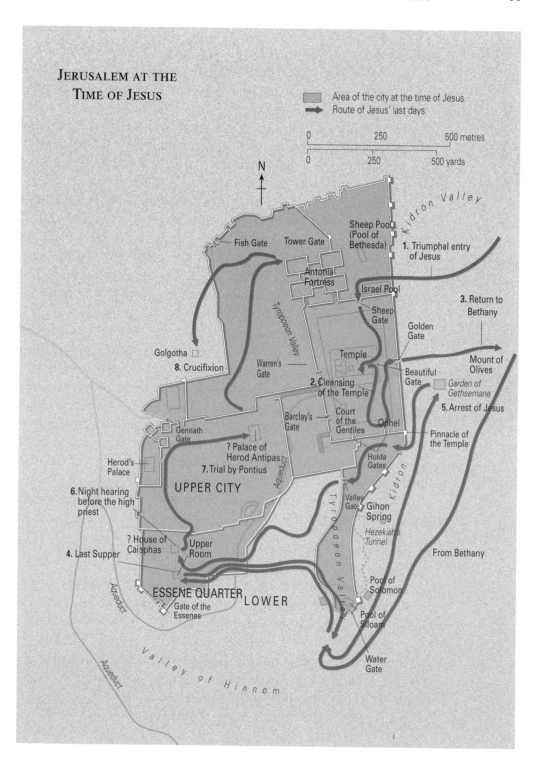

JERUSALEM AT THE
TIME OF JESUS

Area of the city at the time of Jesus
Route of Jesus' last days

0   250   500 metres
0   250   500 yards

N

Kidron Valley

Sheep Pool
(Pool of
Bethesda)

1. Triumphal entry
of Jesus

Fish Gate   Tower Gate

Antonia
Fortress

Israel Pool

3. Return to
Bethany

Sheep
Gate

Tyropoeon Valley

Golden
Gate

Golgotha

8. Crucifixion

Warren's
Gate

Temple

Mount of
Olives

Beautiful
Gate

2. Cleansing
of the Temple

*Garden of
Gethsemane*

5. Arrest of Jesus

Barclay's
Gate

Court
of the
Gentiles

Ophel

Gennath
Gate

Pinnacle of
the Temple

? Palace of
Herod Antipas

7. Trial by Pontius

Hulda
Gates

Herod's
Palace

Aqueduct

UPPER CITY

Valley
Gate

Tyropoeon Valley

Kidron

6. Night hearing
before the high
priest

Gihon
Spring

*Hezekiah's
Tunnel*

? House of
Caiaphas

Upper
Room

From Bethany

4. Last Supper

Aqueduct

ESSENE QUARTER LOWER

Pool of
Solomon

Gate of the
Essenes

Pool of
Siloam

Aqueduct

Water
Gate

Valley of Hinnom

'necessary' for Israel's Messiah* to 'suffer' and 'rise from death three days later', and also for the message about 'repentance and the forgiveness of sins' to be preached to all nations.

Jesus wants us to see two things. First, *that his death was not a mistake* – it was necessary. Three times in Luke 24:46–47, Jesus uses the word 'must' – there was no other way. Jesus' death has been in accordance with God's plan, as already revealed in the Old Testament. So, although Jesus' crucifixion seems like a disaster, instead it is truly a cause for celebration and thanks.

Secondly, *that his death achieved something* – the forgiveness of sins. Because of his death, people from 'all nations' can hear about this offer of forgiveness. But we only receive this forgiveness if we 'repent' – that is, we must be sorry for our sins and turn from them to God. So, because of the cross, people throughout the world are presented with a message about repentance; yet, as they respond, God gives the amazing gift of forgiveness.

Jesus' true followers, then, are those who take seriously Jesus' own teaching about his cross. We accept this vital link between *his* death and *our* sins. We do real business with God, repenting of our sins, and asking truly for his forgiveness. And the Good News is that those who ask truly receive. It is a message about forgiveness – in other words, God really *does* forgive us. God has done everything that is necessary. At the cross, complete forgiveness is guaranteed. Jesus himself wants us to enjoy what he died to achieve.

At the cross, complete forgiveness is guaranteed.

So the second essential building-block in following Jesus is to focus on the cross:

- to know that Jesus' death was no accident, but was God's intended way of bringing forgiveness for sins into his world;
- to recognise that Jesus died for *my* sins – and therefore for *me;*
- to repent before the cross and then to receive what Jesus died to bring us – the assurance of total forgiveness in God's sight.

In other words, it is to *accept Jesus' forgiveness*. So in this chapter we will focus on the cross, learning from the teaching of both Jesus and his apostles concerning what it can mean for us today.

Jesus' own teaching about his death – *before* the event

If you think about it, it is a remarkable thing for anyone to assure another human being that *God* has forgiven them. Who do they think they are? That's precisely what some 'teachers of the Law' asked of Jesus, back at the beginning of his ministry. For, when healing a paralysed man, he outrageously pronounced him to be forgiven. "How does he dare to talk like this?" they asked. "This is blasphemy! God is the only one who can forgive sins!" (Mark 2:7). They were right. Only *God himself* can forgive sins *against God*. But Jesus, because he is God's Son, does have this authority. Through his cross, we begin to see how this can be so. He can declare us forgiven, not only because he is God's Son, but also because he himself has died in our place.

In fact, Jesus had hinted at his forthcoming death for our sins on several occasions long before the event. Consider these verses from Mark's gospel:

- Three times he explicitly predicted his death: "The Son of Man must suffer much and be rejected. ... He will be put to death, but three days later he will rise to life" (8:31; 9:12, 31; 10:33–34).
- He spoke about carrying 'his cross' and predicted (in his parable of the vineyard) that the tenants would kill the owner's 'dear son' (8:34; 12:6).
- He praised a woman for anointing him in advance for his 'burial', and saw his death as predicted in the Old Testament: "the Son of Man will die as the Scriptures say he will" (14:8, 21, 27, 49).
- At the Last Supper, he spoke of his body being broken and his blood "poured out for many" (14:22–23).
- He summarised the whole purpose of his coming in these powerful words: "the Son of Man ... came to serve and to give his life to redeem [or ransom] many people" (10:45).

So, even if his followers needed this to be explained all over again after the event, Jesus himself had been quite clear beforehand. Yes, Jesus had other reasons for going up to Jerusalem – speaking out as a prophet before his national leaders, challenging the Temple with his own authority, and staking his claim in the capital to be the true 'king of the Jews'. But he also went up to Jerusalem knowing it would end in agony. He would give his life, and his death would be an act of redemption, to bring God's forgiveness and freedom to many people. Jesus' followers take him at his word.

The apostles' subsequent teaching

The apostles expand on Jesus' teaching. In fact, they are always talking about the cross. They therefore talk about it in many different ways, but the heart of their message is always the same:

- Jesus' death was 'for our sins' (1 Corinthians 15:3).
- His death was unlike any other death; it was not an accident but all part of God's purpose and plan (Acts 4:28).
- Jesus had not died because of his own sins – indeed they make the remarkable claim that he had *no sin of his own* (1 John 3:5, 1 Peter 2:22; Hebrews 4:15). No, it was because of *our* sins (Romans 8:3; Hebrews 10:18; 13:12).

The New Testament writers use different pictures to explain this great event (see Box 2a). It is worth pausing and giving this material our full attention. As we do so, these pictures may appear slightly complex. Yet, remember, the New Testament writers were dealing here with the most extraordinary event in the world, so it should not be surprising if their teaching pushes us to the limits of human language. What pictures can really be adequate to convey such a unique event?

Box 2a – Four apostolic images to explain the cross

BROKEN FAMILY RELATIONSHIPS

The first is drawn from the world of personal relationships. Because of our sins, there was a barrier between us and God (e.g. Isaiah 59:2), but now, through Jesus' death, that barrier has been removed. At the time of Jesus' death, the Temple curtain, which separated worshippers from the Most Holy Place, was dramatically 'torn in two, from top to bottom' (Mark 15:38); this can be taken as a sign that the barrier of sin has been removed and we can now enter into God's holy presence (as argued in Hebrews 10:19–22). As a result, we can come running back into the arms of our heavenly Father: thus the 'lost son' in Jesus' parable found a generous welcome (Luke 15:11–32). For this new welcome, the apostles use the language of reconciliation and peace, of friendship instead of enmity:

God ... through Christ changed us from enemies into his friends. ... God was making the whole human race his friends through Christ. God did not keep an account of their sins ...

2 CORINTHIANS 5:18–19

At one time you were far away from God and were his enemies because of the evil things you did and thought. But now, by means of the physical death of his Son, God has made you his friends ...

COLOSSIANS 1:21–22

THE SLAVE MARKET

In the second image, human beings are presented as being like slaves, but by his death Jesus paid a great price for us, which purchased our freedom – we can be free! For this, the apostles use the language of 'redemption' (literally, a 'buying back'), which is similar in its meanings to the word 'ransom':

By the blood of Christ we are set free, that is, our sins are forgiven.

EPHESIANS 1:7
(SEE ALSO MARK 10:45; 1 PETER 1:18; 1 TIMOTHY 2:6; ROMANS 3:24; TITUS 2:14)

THE LAW COURTS

The third image is a legal one. We were guilty and had received a death sentence from God, but Jesus died in our place and we can now walk away from the court as free people – not guilty! For this, the apostles use the language of 'justification' and righteousness; we are 'justified' in God's sight (that is, 'put right' with him) through the death of Jesus, who himself was truly faithful and righteous:

[God] deals with their sins, in order to demonstrate his righteousness. In this way God shows that he himself is righteous and that he puts right everyone who believes in Jesus.

ROMANS 3:25–26 (SEE ALSO GALATIANS 2:16–17; 3:24)

By becoming a curse for us Christ has redeemed us from the curse that the Law brings ...

GALATIANS 3:13

I no longer have a righteousness of my own. ... I now have the righteousness ... that comes from God and is based on faith.

PHILIPPIANS 3:9

THE JERUSALEM TEMPLE

Finally, the apostles draw upon the image of the Temple – the place appointed by God for the offering of special sacrifices to remove the sins of his people. Jesus' death, the apostles teach, is the one, true sacrifice, which has truly turned aside God's wrath – we can be counted holy in God's sight and enter his presence. For this, they use the language of 'propitiation', 'atonement', 'sacrifice' and often refer to Jesus' crucifixion by talking of his 'blood', thereby emphasising its sacrificial purpose (see Acts 20:28; Colossians 1:14; Hebrews 9:14; Revelation 1:5). These words may seem alien to us today but would have been very familiar to people who knew the Old Testament Temple:

- God's wrath was now 'propitiated' or 'turned aside', not by the sacrifice of an animal in the Temple, but by 'the costly sacrifice of Christ, who was like a lamb without defect or flaw' (1 Peter 1:19; see also John 1:29; Romans 3:24; 1 Corinthians 5:7; 1 John 2:2; Revelation 5:6, 9). This sacrifice atoned for our sins, covering them over in such a way that God no longer needs to consider them any more.
- '[Christ] offered himself as a perfect sacrifice to God ... to remove sin through the sacrifice of himself' (Hebrews 9:14, 26; see also Hebrews 10:10).

The heart of the cross

In the light of this New Testament teaching, we can deduce several important points, which will take us to the heart of what was going on at the cross.

1. The apostles always link the cross with our 'sins'

For them, Jesus' death is not just an example of heroic suffering or powerful love. Of course, it is a great act of love, but only because it achieved something for us – it did something to our sins. In one key verse, Peter refers to Jesus' 'sin-bearing', which (in the light of its Old Testament usage) means receiving the penalty that our sins deserved:

> *Christ himself carried our sins in his body to the cross...*
>
> 1 PETER 2:24

It is an act of *salvation** which brings us into a place of safety. The very name 'Jesus' means 'God saves' (Matthew 1:21) and there are frequent references to him as the 'Saviour'. He 'came into the world to save sinners' (1 Timothy 1:15).

Sometimes we dislike this emphasis on sin. Do we really have to see Jesus' death against this background? What if our sinfulness is not so serious? And, anyway, couldn't God forgive us without anyone needing to die for us? Yet this overlooks the seriousness of sin in God's sight. Note four key points that Paul makes in Romans concerning the seriousness of sin (Romans 2:11; 3:23; 5:12; 6:23):

- God judges everyone by the same standard.
- Everyone has sinned and is far away from God's saving presence.
- Death has spread to the whole human race because everyone has sinned.
- Sin pays its wages – death.

Sin is thus a more deadly disease than we know. Jesus knew this. He too warned people they would "die in their sins" (John 8:21, 24). That's why he gave his life, to rescue us from the death that will come to us because of our sins. If, instead, we pretend that sin is unimportant, we imply that Jesus' death was pointless. It's a brave person who says that to Jesus.

2. The apostles understand that Jesus did something for us which we could never do for ourselves

It is not as though, with a little more effort, we could have made our own way back to God or worked out our own salvation. No, there is the frank realisation that we are inept, helpless, and unable to save ourselves.

> *When we were still helpless, Christ died for the wicked; ... it was while we were still sinners that Christ died for us!*
>
> ROMANS 5:6, 8

As a result, 'it is by God's grace that you have been saved through faith. It is not the result of your own efforts' (Ephesians 2:8–9). So we should not think of Jesus just as our *representative* (doing something for us, as it were, as our leader) but rather as our *substitute* (doing something in our place and on our behalf, which we ourselves could never do). Jesus gave his life *for* us; but, when pressed, that little word 'for' strictly means 'in our place' or 'instead of us'.

3. The apostles express their wonder that on the cross this was *God himself* at work

The New Testament writers are adamant that the cross is the work of God. Jesus is not some poor human being – an innocent third party – whom God asks to die for others. No, in Jesus' death on the cross, God himself was showing his own love for us.

So Paul writes, '*God* has shown us how much he loves us when ... *Christ* died for us' (Romans 5:8). Look at this verse very carefully: it only makes sense if Christ and God are identified in some way. If they were quite separate, then the cross would only show us the love of *Christ*, not the love of *God*. But in fact, the cross does show us God's love, because Christ was there acting *for* and *as* God. As Paul says, God was acting directly in and through Christ – 'the full content of divine nature lives in Christ' (Colossians 2:9; see also 2 Corinthians 5:19).

> In Jesus' death on the cross, God himself was showing his own love for us.

This is truly amazing. In what other religion does God love us so much as to ... die for us? Look how much he gave up for us so that we might be forgiven! Effectively, if Jesus was our substitute, then we must now say that *God himself substituted himself for us*. In other words, when faced with the cross, we are looking at an act of *divine self-sacrifice*:

- 'Christ was without sin, but for our sake God made him share our sin in order that in union with him we might share the righteousness of God' (2 Corinthians 5:21).
- 'God loved the world so much that he gave his only Son' (John 3:16).

Truly, salvation is won for us, not by human beings, but only by the Lord himself. This is well expressed in the Old Testament: 'Salvation comes from the LORD!' (Jonah 2:9). No one else can save us but God alone, and, through Jesus' cross, that is precisely what God has done.

Jesus' followers, then, should never move away from the cross. They should never dismiss it as elementary or primitive – something which they can now leave behind because they are too mature or have no need for it. On the contrary, we should return to it on a daily basis – this is the only place where we can safely stand before God. All other ground is shifting sand.

So the cross is the bedrock of our faith. It may seem 'foolish' and 'weak' to others, Paul notes, but to us it is 'the power of God and the wisdom of God' (1 Corinthians 1:24). Paul himself focused his teaching on 'Christ crucified' and wanted others to fill their imaginations with the cross (1 Corinthians 2:2; Galatians 3:1). In his experience it was the only thing that a believer should ever boast about:

> I will boast only about the cross of our Lord Jesus Christ...
> GALATIANS 6:14 (SEE ALSO 1 CORINTHIANS 1:18–31)

Coming to the cross

The cross, then, is God's greatest action in human history. Not surprisingly, therefore, we see hints of it way back in the Old Testament – as God prepared his people for the coming of his great salvation.

That's why, on the Emmaus road, we saw Jesus pointing out 'from all the Scriptures' that it was 'necessary for the Messiah to suffer' (Luke 24:26–27). He wanted them to put the jigsaw together, to see how the cross was the goal of God's long-term purposes. Almost certainly, at some point, he will have drawn attention to the so-called 'Servant Songs' in the prophecy of Isaiah. The last of these (amazingly, written over 500 years earlier) predicts in an uncanny way the events of Jesus' crucifixion. It is worth reading all of Isaiah 52:13 – 53:12. The

Lord's Servant, it says, would be 'despised', 'rejected' and brought down to death, but this would come about, not because of his own sins, but because of the sins of others:

> But because of **our** sins **he** was wounded,
>   beaten because of the evil **we** did.
> **We** are healed by the punishment **he** suffered,
>   made whole by the blows **he** received.
> All of us were like sheep that were lost,
>   each of us going his own way.
> But the Lord made the punishment fall on **him**,
>   the punishment all of **us** deserved.
>
> Isaiah 53:5–6

Here again, we see the way the Bible links between sin and death. Here is someone suffering for the sins of others, receiving the punishment they deserved. This prophecy then explains Peter's clear vision (above p.39) of the cross as the place of 'sin-bearing', as well as Jesus' own reference to his life being given 'to redeem many people' (Mark 10:45; 1 Peter 2:24). Reading this prophecy prayerfully and faithfully, Jesus would have realised that he himself was called to be the Suffering Servant of the Lord (though paradoxically, as we have seen, he was also the Lord himself!).

Yet Isaiah's prophecy also speaks clearly about *us*. 'All of us,' it says, 'were like sheep that were lost.' In relation to God, we do indeed wander like sheep: we dislike his rule, cherish our independence and go off and do our own thing. This wandering and disobedience is part of what the Bible refers to as 'sin' – a short word for what is a huge problem. In God's sight, 'everyone has sinned and, as a result, is far way from God's saving presence' (Romans 3:23; see also 3:9–12). Is there any way back?

The cross of Jesus is God's answer. It is the place where 'we are healed', the place where sin is dealt with once and for all, the place where the barrier between us and God is decisively removed. For (as Isaiah foresaw) the Lord, the holy God of Israel, 'made the punishment, which all of us deserved, to fall on him' – that is, on Jesus, his Son. This removes our sins, as it were, from off our shoulders and onto Christ's; and it therefore removes the barrier of sin between us and God. The possibility of intimate relationship with God is restored.

As a result (to use a different picture), Jesus' death then becomes like a bridge from earth to heaven, from human beings to God – it is the one way through to God (see the bridge diagram on p. 102). As Peter says: 'Christ died for sins once and for all, a good man on behalf of sinners, in order to lead you to God' (1 Peter 3:18). Through the cross, the barrier is brought down and the road opened for travel – all we now need to do is to walk along it!

So, if we want to approach God with a clear conscience with all barriers broken down, and if we want to be declared 'not guilty' and included in God's family, then we must come to Jesus at his cross. We must place our sins on him, asking Jesus to carry them for us; we must repent, asking God for his forgiveness.

In God's sight, people's sins are located in one of two places: either on the shoulders of the person who has committed them, or on Jesus who offers to carry them. We have to ask ourselves: where now are our sins? Through the cross, Jesus wants to take this major burden off our shoulders. Indeed people cannot follow Jesus if they insist on carrying their own burdens along the road. Instead we each need to confess our sins and then give them over to Jesus.

What happens when we do this? Here is what the New Testament promises:

- We are forgiven: 'I will no longer remember their wrongs' (Hebrews 8:12, quoting Jeremiah 31:34).
- We are reckoned as righteous (or justified) in God's sight, 'put right with him' and vindicated in God's court of judgement (Romans 3:24; 5:1).
- We have 'peace with God' (Romans 5:1).
- We are 'adopted' as God's own children into his family; those who receive Jesus in this way are given by him the 'right to become God's children' (John 1:12; see also Romans 8:15–17; Ephesians 1:5; Galatians 3:26).
- We can now dare to call Almighty God 'our Father' (as Jesus encourages us in the Lord's Prayer) and enjoy a personal relationship with him – so personal, in fact, that the Bible even uses the word 'Abba'* (which means 'my dad'; see Matthew 6:9; Galatians 4:6; Romans 8:15; and below, chapter 3).
- We become full members of the people of God (Galatians 4:7; Ephesians 2:19; Romans 3:29–30).

These are the great New Testament promises that apply to us – but only because of Jesus' cross. We may sometimes feel they are not true, but our feelings are unreliable guides – what is utterly reliable is Jesus' cross. This event is an unchangeable event in human history. God cannot, as it were, *undo what he has done*. So we should build our lives on this solid rock. We should take God at his word and humbly receive what he promises: total forgiveness.

So the second building-block in the Christian life is to understand the cross and to *enjoy God's forgiveness*. In some ways, this could have been our first building-block. For, when individuals first come to Jesus, they must always know their need for his forgiveness, hence the reference to Jesus' death in the sample prayer (see p. 29). Even so, it was helpful in chapter 1 to focus on the resurrection, because without the resurrection, Jesus' cross lacks any power. The cross on its own – without the resurrection – is only half the story. After all, a Jesus who stays dead is ultimately no Good News at all.

> *Everyone needs to move on to discover the other half of the story: the Risen Jesus also died for us; and the one who died for us is alive today.*

But as soon as we affirm Jesus' resurrection, we see the cross in a whole new light: as God's appointed sacrifice, gladly accepted, and as the moment of Jesus' greatest glory – where he won a resounding victory over evil and the powers of darkness (John 12:23; 2 Corinthians 13:4; Colossians 2:15).

So the cross and the resurrection belong together. Some people may find that they first come to Christ through pondering the truth of the resurrection, others through hearing about the cross. But everyone needs to move on to discover the other half of the story: the Risen Jesus also died for us; and the one who died for us is alive today.

> *I am the living one! I was dead, but now I am alive for ever and ever.*
>
> REVELATION 1:18

Living under the cross

So this is where our Christian life begins – at the cross of the Risen Jesus. If it does not begin here, it does not begin at all. Yet, in a sense, this is also where we must stay throughout our Christian lives. As we have seen, we can never say 'goodbye' to the cross, or move on to seemingly more important things.

In chapter 11 we will explore further what it means in practice to keep living under the cross in our fight against sin in our lives. For now, however, we close by noting simply how the cross can help us to be sure of God's love for us.

In our early days as Jesus' followers, we often have many doubts. What if I keep sinning? Am I really 'saved'? Am I part of God's family? We keep feeling we have failed too badly or have not been committed enough. God knows all this, but he encourages us to keep coming back to the cross.

- He wants us to realise that Jesus died for *all* our sin – no sin is so terrible that somehow Jesus did not die for *that* sin.
- He wants us to see that Jesus *loves us totally*. Even if we had been the only person in the world, he would still have died for me: he is 'the Son of God, who loved me and gave his life for me' (Galatians 2:20).

So we are not to worry whether we are good enough. Instead, we can have a humble assurance, both that we now truly belong to God and also that we will go to be with him when we die. He is now fully committed to us, and Jesus is 'pleading with God' for us, because our names are 'written' in the 'book of life' (Hebrews 7:25; Revelation 13:8). Indeed Jesus the Good Shepherd knows each of his followers 'by name' and has promised that "no one can snatch them away from me" (John 10:28).

So, when we continue to sin against God – as we will each day – we must learn to return to the cross. The apostle John, in assuring young Christians, proclaimed that believers had truly 'passed from death to life' and would 'not be judged' (John 5:24). Yet he knew we would continue to sin. So he wisely wrote:

> The blood of Jesus, God's Son, purifies us from every sin.
> If we say that we have no sin, we deceive ourselves, and there is no truth in us. But if we confess our sins to God, he will keep his promise and do what is right: he will forgive us our sins and purify us from all our wrongdoing.
>
> 1 John 1:7–9

Every day, we need God's forgiveness. And every day we can receive it through the cross. 'The Lord's unfailing love and mercy still continue – fresh as the morning, as sure as the sunrise' (Lamentations 3:22–23). So the second building-block in the Christian life is to keep coming to the cross of Jesus – to *accept his forgiveness* and to receive his love.

Building-block 2

Accept His Forgiveness – Jesus Died for You!

Welcome His Spirit

"I myself will send upon you what my Father has promised."

LUKE 24:49

Luke 24 describes one long, memorable day — the first Easter Sunday. It was a day full of surprises, from dawn till dusk: visions of angels, strange encounters on the road, and an in-depth Bible study with an unrecognised teacher. But before the day was out, Jesus' followers were in for another surprise. 'I myself will send upon you what my Father has promised,' Jesus said. 'But you must wait in the city until the power from above comes down upon you.' Jesus' followers would be given a special gift — the gift of the Holy Spirit.

After focusing on his death and resurrection, what was the very next thing Jesus wanted his followers to understand? Answer: the Holy Spirit. Although the word 'Spirit' is not expressly used in Luke 24, this 'promised gift' from the Father clearly refers to the Holy Spirit. We know this because the opening chapters of Luke's second volume tell us the story of what happened next — when the Holy Spirit came in power (see Acts 2, printed in full on pages 106). Ten days later, Jesus' followers, following his instructions, are indeed waiting in the city of Jerusalem. Then suddenly there is a great noise like that of 'a strong wind blowing' and they are 'all filled with the Holy Spirit'. The Holy Spirit has come upon them.

We call this event Pentecost*****. It marked the launch of Jesus' church. It was a clear, unrepeatable sign that Jesus' people from now on will always be people of the Spirit. We shall be looking at this event in more detail in part 2, but for now we focus on this earlier promise of Jesus concerning the Holy Spirit in Luke 24. We shall find his words open up for us a surprising new sphere of spiritual reality.

What would we think if someone came up to us in the street and said something like this: "I am going to live *inside* you!"? We would say they were mad. How can anyone live inside someone else? But Jesus can – and he does! This turns out to be what the promised gift of the Holy Spirit is all about. Jesus lives within each of his followers by means of the Holy Spirit.

So the third building-block in following Jesus will be all about welcoming this Holy Spirit within our lives, for the Spirit is the very life of Jesus himself within us. From now on, we are never alone; following Jesus need never be something we do in our own strength. No, we find we have a new engine inside: his powerful Spirit.

Jesus teaches his followers about the coming Holy Spirit

What is the basis for this seemingly bizarre idea that Jesus can somehow live within us? Or that the Holy Spirit can be identified in some way with Jesus himself? The answer, once again, is that Jesus himself expressly taught this amazing truth.

A few days earlier, on the night before he died, Jesus had said these puzzling words:

> "Those who love me will obey my teaching. My Father and I will come to them and dwell within each one of them."
>
> JOHN 14:23

Back in chapter 1, we saw how the Risen Jesus sees the believer's life as a house, and he promises to 'come in', when he is asked. Here Jesus is using the same picture and making the same promise: he will come into the home of our lives and he will live within us. But in this passage, three new things stand out about Jesus' promise:

- Jesus emphasises that he will be taking up a *fixed* residence. He will not be leaving again suddenly, but he will be dwelling (or abiding) with us. We become, as it were, his permanent home!
- God the Father also comes to reside within the believer.
- Jesus makes it clear that this is the work of the Holy Spirit. It will be by means of the Holy Spirit that God and Jesus are able to live within the believer.

Box 3a – Jesus' teaching about the Holy Spirit at the Last Supper

"I will ask the Father, and he will give you another Helper, who will stay with you for ever. He is the Spirit who reveals the truth about God. The world cannot receive him, because it cannot see him or know him. But you know him, because he remains with you and is in you.

When I go, you will not be left all alone; I will come back to you.

The Helper, the Holy Spirit, whom the Father will send in my name, will teach you everything.

The Helper will come – the Spirit, who reveals the truth about God – and he will speak about me.

Your hearts are full of sadness. But I am telling you the truth: it is better for you that I go away, because if I do not go, the Helper will not come to you. But if I do go away, then I will send him to you. And when he comes, he will prove to the people of the world that they are wrong about sin and about what is right and about God's judgement. ...

When, however, the Spirit comes, who reveals the truth about God, he will lead you into all the truth. He will not speak on his own authority, but he will speak of what he hears, and will tell you of things to come. He will give me glory, because he will take what I say and tell it to you."

JOHN 14:16–18, 26; 15:26; 16:6–8, 13–14

From Jesus' other teaching on that night (see Box 3a), we see how Jesus is preparing his followers for his own imminent departure and death. They must not be sad, because he will 'come back' to them. But when we ask how (or in what way) Jesus is coming back, the answer from these verses is clear: *by the Holy Spirit*. When the Holy Spirit comes to them, this will be *Jesus* coming back to them.

That's why Jesus describes the Holy Spirit as 'another Helper'. That word 'another' literally means 'another one *of the same kind*'. Just as Jesus was the great Helper, so the Holy Spirit will be. What Jesus is, the Holy Spirit is. God is not sending someone completely different from Jesus – but another one, just like him!

> When the Holy Spirit comes to them, this will be Jesus coming back to them.

Jesus also teaches here several other important truths about the Holy Spirit:

- He is able to reveal God's truths to his people.
- He is able to convict people in the 'world' of their sin.
- He is to be thought of as a Person, not just an impersonal force, because he is 'another', like Jesus. Since Jesus was a person, so the Holy Spirit is too.
- Unlike Jesus, who was confined to one physical location, the Spirit may dwell in many different people – as many as believe in Jesus – all around the world.
- He is an unseen reality that unbelievers cannot see, know or understand. This means there is indeed 'more to life than meets the eye'. The physical, visible world is not the sum of all reality. The Spirit is an unseen but nevertheless real personal power at work in the world.

> The Spirit is an unseen but nevertheless real personal power at work in the world.

The most important point, however, is this: Jesus is able to live within his people by the Holy Spirit. If we are now believers in Jesus, then the Holy Spirit truly lives within us!

The Holy Spirit in the New Testament

In due course, Jesus' followers discovered exactly what he meant. The Holy Spirit came upon them at Pentecost. And then the same things happened for those to whom they preached. These people too discovered this great reality of the Spirit. They had never seen Jesus physically, but they knew him by his Spirit – and his Spirit truly dwelt within them.

Read the book of Acts to see just how the Holy Spirit spread. See what the first Christians were able to accomplish because of Jesus' Spirit within them! Some people have suggested that 'The Acts of the Apostles' (the normal, full title of Luke's second volume) should instead be called 'The Acts of Jesus', or 'The Acts of the Holy Spirit'. For truly, what we are seeing there is the incredible outworking of Jesus' own life and power through the agency of his Spirit. The Mediterranean world of the first century was hit by a tidal wave of spiritual power and energy, the ripples from which can still be sensed today. And what was the cause of the ripples? Nothing less than the Spirit-empowered life of Jesus, now unleashed on the world through Jesus' Spirit being at work within his followers.

So the New Testament writers often speak about the Holy Spirit (see Box 3b) – and they do so very much from personal experience. This is no merely academic matter, but a profound, life-changing reality, which you too can enjoy. Ask any Christian and they ought to be able to speak about the Holy Spirit at work in their lives.

Box 3b – The apostles' teaching on the Holy Spirit: Three great realities

1. THE HOLY SPIRIT IS A PERSON

He is not an 'it', nor an impersonal force. He is an eternal Person within the Godhead. So the New Testament writers speak of God as 'the Father, the Son, and the Holy Spirit' (Matthew 28:19).

2. THE HOLY SPIRIT IS THE POWER OF GOD

The few Old Testament references to the Spirit use the language of God's 'breath' (Hebrew: *ruach*). It is by his 'breath' that God speaks his powerful Word in creation, and by his Spirit he inspires the ancient prophets of Israel (Psalm 33:4–7; 2 Peter 1:21). In the New Testament. Jesus himself is the human being who is 'full of the Holy Spirit' (Luke 4:1, 14), and by his Spirit his followers sometimes perform powerful deeds and miracles (Hebrews 2:4; Acts 3:8; 5:9; 13:11; 19:11–12; 28:8). This power of the Holy Spirit is seen, perhaps supremely, in the 'miracle' of conversion. Every time someone puts their faith in Christ, this is directly the work of the Holy Spirit, who has been convicting that person, speaking to them and drawing them towards Christ (John 16:8–11; see also 1 Corinthians 12:3). Moreover, the 'new birth' that results is also evidence of the Spirit's power (John 3:3–6).

3. THE HOLY SPIRIT IS THE PRESENCE OF GOD

God the Father dwells in his majesty and holiness beyond and above our world, yet he is also able to be present *within* our world by his Spirit. Old Testament believers sensed God's presence in Jerusalem's

Temple – it was the 'dwelling place of God's Name'. In the New Testament, however, Jesus, as God incarnate*, was God's presence on earth; this means he has replaced the Temple with himself (see Deuteronomy 12:11; Psalm 26:8; John 1:14; 2:19–21). He has also made his church to be a temple; and we ourselves as believers are, as it were, miniature temples (1 Corinthians 3:16; 6:19). This means that God is now present in his world – through living within you and me!

God is offering us this very special gift. To be a Christian is not just about knowing Jesus because of his resurrection; nor just about receiving God's forgiveness through the cross. God has a third great gift for us: We can enjoy God's empowering presence within our lives through the Person of the Holy Spirit.

Common questions

This teaching about the Holy Spirit may leave us, however, with some real questions.

The Spirit within – picture or reality?

Is this talk of the Holy Spirit 'living within us' really true? Or is it just a picture? Perhaps it is just a colourful way of speaking? After all, we cannot *see* the Holy Spirit. So where exactly in our bodies – within our persons – is he supposed to be living?

People in Jesus' day struggled with just this kind of question. We see this in the way a man called Nicodemus responded to some of Jesus' earlier teaching about the Holy Spirit. Jesus had said to him:

> "You hear the sound the wind makes, but you do not know where it comes from or where it is going. It is like that with everyone who is born of the Spirit."
>
> JOHN 3:8

Understandably, Nicodemus had replied, "How can this be?" It doesn't seem to make sense! We feel comfortable with what we can see, but we cannot see the Holy Spirit. Nevertheless, just because the Spirit is invisible – like the wind, says Jesus – this does not mean he is not real.

In his later teaching (see Box 3a), Jesus was quite clear that people in the 'world' (that is, people who do not believe in Jesus) will simply never understand the reality of the Holy Spirit: "The world cannot receive him". Yet their unbelief or cynicism does not deny the Spirit's reality. Jesus went on:

> "But you know him, because he remains with you and is in you."
>
> JOHN 14:17

In other words, believers in Jesus will be able to sense his reality.

As to where exactly the Spirit resides within us, perhaps the best way to understand the Bible's teaching is to think of the Spirit dwelling *within our 'spirits'*. Paul hints at this when he writes: 'though your body is dead because of sin, your spirit is alive because of righteousness' (Romans 8:10, my translation). When we believe in Jesus, it is our spirits within us, which previously were dead, that now come alive – presumably by the operation and presence of God's Spirit within them. We may not see anything, but God is truly present within our spirits. This is not just a picture, however. This is an *unseen spiritual reality*.

The Spirit's permanence — in every believer?

Is it really true that every believer has the Holy Spirit? Perhaps the Holy Spirit is only for good Christians? Perhaps only for those with special, 'miraculous' gifts? Perhaps he comes and goes – sometimes being present within the believer, sometimes not?

Despite what many people say, the New Testament is crystal clear about this. The Holy Spirit dwells within each believer from the moment that person first believes in Jesus – and he never leaves! Yes, we may often grieve him (Ephesians 4:30) and we are encouraged to keep on being 'filled with the Spirit' (Ephesians 5:18); yet the Holy Spirit never leaves us. Nor does he wait till we have become mature or seemingly 'powerful' Christians. We see this teaching in many places:

> *The Holy Spirit dwells within each believer from the moment that person first believes in Jesus – and he never leaves!*

- As we have already seen, when people open their lives to him, the Risen Jesus says, "I will come in" and promises to stay or live in them for ever (Revelation 3:20; John 14:16, 23). He remains in us and we become his permanent address. Jesus keeps his promises. These verses do not say, "I will be leaving again very soon afterwards"!

- Paul too teaches very clearly: 'Whoever does not have the Spirit of Christ does not belong to him' (Romans 8:9–10). By implication, therefore, if we *do* belong to him, then we *do* have the Holy Spirit. We cannot be Christ's without his Spirit. So Paul goes on to affirm quite clearly for these believers: 'Christ lives in you'.

We are not to doubt that the Holy Spirit is now truly within us. If we have put our trust in Jesus as our Lord and Saviour, if we have asked him to come into our lives, then *from that moment* the Holy Spirit lives within us. (There is only one episode in the New Testament which suggests that some believers experienced something slightly different, namely, when the Good News first reached the Samaritans*.) We may not always feel this, but it is a fact. And we must begin to build our lives on this amazing spiritual reality: *we are God-indwelt people!*

We will need to claim this great truth against our own doubting, perhaps when we feel far from God or know we have sinned against him; perhaps too when we see other believers acting in ways that dishonour God, or even hurting us in some way. Whatever we may think, the Spirit is still within them, though he may well be grieving over the situation and their behaviour. The Spirit does not, as it were, come and go, but is rather the Spirit who abides and stays put.

Spiritual 'gifts' — all of them for everyone?

There is another situation in which we may need to claim this truth even more. This is when we encounter people who seem 'super-spiritual' – those people who imply that we cannot have the Holy Spirit in our lives because we don't do all the 'spiritual things' that they do (speaking in tongues*, performing miracles, leading powerful worship or whatever it may be).

These spiritual things are often referred to as spiritual gifts* and Paul in 1 Corinthians 12–14 encourages us to seek after them: 'Set your hearts on spiritual gifts' (1 Corinthians 14:1). Yet he is also aware that they can cause great arguments and divisions amongst people. That's why he says the most important spiritual gift is love (1 Corinthians 13:1–13). We are certainly not acting in love if we cause young Christians to doubt the presence of the Holy Spirit in their lives by drawing attention to our own supposedly greater gifting! So Paul teaches here that no believer is without some kind of spiritual gift.

> The Spirit's presence is shown in some way in each person for the good of all.
>
> 1 CORINTHIANS 12:7

Paul wants us to recognise that it is the Spirit, not we ourselves, who gives these gifts – 'as he wishes, he gives a different gift to each person' (12:11). He also stresses that they are always given for 'the good of all' (12:7) and that no individual possesses *all* the gifts. Instead, just as a body has many different parts, so believers have a variety of gifts – with each person's gifts complementing the gifts of others.

So, by all means, ask God for more of the Spirit; yes, seek spiritual gifts. But also be wary of those people who draw attention to their own gifts. Above all, never doubt that the Holy Spirit is already within you. And, if ever we find ourselves asking God for (more of) the Spirit, let us remember that we are not asking the Spirit, as though he were absent, *to come for the first time*. No, we are asking the Spirit, who is already present through our faith in Jesus, simply to *reveal more* of his presence and power in our lives.

Learning from the Spirit

Jesus wants us to follow him by drawing upon the help of his Holy Spirit, who now lives within us. Here, then, are four key points we should remember about the Spirit's purpose as we get used to living under his direction. What does the Holy Spirit want?

1. The Holy Spirit always wants to point us towards Jesus

Jesus said of the Holy Spirit: "He will give me glory" (John 16:14). The Holy Spirit is fixated with the glory of Jesus and wants us to appreciate this glory for ourselves. So, if we want to cooperate with the Spirit, this means we will keep our eyes fixed on Jesus and seek to promote his glory and praise. It means letting the Holy Spirit show us more of Jesus. The Spirit-filled life will always be a Jesus-focused life.

> The Holy Spirit is fixated with the glory of Jesus.

2. The Holy Spirit wants us to enjoy our relationship with God as our Father

Paul writes:

> Those who are led by God's Spirit are God's children. For the Spirit ... makes you God's children, and by the Spirit's power we cry out to God, "Father! my Father!"
>
> ROMANS 8:14–15

Indeed he goes on: 'God's Spirit joins himself to our spirits to declare that we are God's children' (8:16). In Galatians he says the same: 'To show that you are his sons and daughters, God sent the Spirit of his Son into our hearts, the Spirit who cries out, "Father, my Father"' (Galatians 4:6). The Spirit wants us to dare to call God our 'Father'.

For some of us, this may be incredibly difficult. We cannot think of God in this intimate way; indeed we often find it hard to believe he is interested in us at all. For some of us, this may be partly because of our relationship with our own, human father. Many of us come from families where our fathers have been removed from us – through their over-busyness or emotional distance, through divorce or their death; and some, sadly, have had abusive fathers. Few of us know the liberating power of a father's love for us. But this is where the Good News kicks in! Each of us who believes in Jesus now has the living God for our true Father.

> The Spirit wants us to dare to call God our 'Father'.

The Holy Spirit wants to help us sense our Father's love for us, to know deep down his unique delight in us as his children. He wants us to hear addressed to us the same words as God once spoke to Jesus: "You are my own dear Son. I am pleased with you" (Mark 1:11). Jesus was God's 'Child' in a unique sense, but we too are now truly God's children through being 'adopted' into his family (Romans 8:15, 23; Galatians 4:5). Jesus has given us 'the right to become God's children' (John 1:12; see also 20:17). God wants us to run like a little child into his arms, crying out, "Abba*, Dad!" Jesus' followers, because of the Spirit, are to walk through each day knowing they are truly children of their heavenly Father, looking up to his face, and drawing into their inmost beings his deep delight.

3. The Holy Spirit wants to help us to pray

Paul continues:

> The Spirit also comes to help us, weak as we are. For we do not know how we ought to pray; the Spirit himself pleads with God for us in groans that words cannot express.
>
> ROMANS 8:26

None of us, naturally, finds it easy to pray. But now that the Holy Spirit is actually residing within us, he can help us. Focused times of prayer can become opportunities when we let the Spirit within us do the praying. And our whole lives can be lived 'in the Spirit' as we 'pray on every occasion, as the Spirit leads' (Ephesians 6:18).

4. The Holy Spirit wants to enable us to live like Jesus

When we first believe in Jesus, we come to him as Saviour, because we recognise God's judgement upon our human sin. We renounce evil and choose now to go God's way. After that, the Christian life is meant to continue in the same vein – an ongoing and continual turning away from sin. But how can we do this? We may have good intentions, but we are all so weak!

This is where the Spirit comes to our rescue. For not only can the Spirit reveal to us what Jesus would do; he can also then give us the strength to do it. We will return to this key point in chapter 10, but for now we note that this is perhaps the most important of the Spirit's desires – to help us live as Jesus would want us to. This dependency on God's Spirit will need to become a daily feature of our lives.

This dependency on God's Spirit will need to become a daily feature of our lives.

Every believer in Jesus has the Spirit of Jesus within them. All of us must learn to love Jesus' Spirit, recognising his presence with us, and walking each day in his power and strength. The third key building-block for growing as a Christian is to *welcome God's Spirit* daily – for already, through our faith in Jesus, he is living within us.

As we look back over these first three chapters, we can sense what a great foundation we have been given in the Good News:

- In chapter 1 we saw how God is now *with* us: because of the resurrection, Jesus is alive today and able to meet with us.
- In chapter 2 we saw that God is *for* us: because of Jesus' cross, we can now be God's friends, forgiven and holy in his sight.
- Now in chapter 3 we see that God is also *in* us: because the Holy Spirit is given to *every* believer in Jesus Christ.

God with us, God for us, God in us! Now there's a slogan worth remembering – perhaps reciting to yourself every morning. These great truths are a solid, immoveable foundation on which we can build our Christian lives.

Building-block 3

Welcome His Spirit
– Jesus Lives in You!

4

Feed on His Scriptures

Jesus explained to them what was said about himself in all the Scriptures. ...

They said to each other, "Wasn't it like a fire burning in us while he ... explained the Scriptures to us?"

LUKE 24:25, 27, 32

The Risen Jesus is laying down good foundations for his followers. He teaches about the three great realities at the heart of Christian faith (his resurrection, the cross and the Spirit), but there is more. On several occasions during that first Easter Day, as recorded in Luke 24, he draws the attention of his followers to the importance of something else: the Holy Scriptures.

The Scriptures (literally, the 'writings') were what we now call the 'Old Testament'. They were ancient texts, received by God's people through the centuries, in which they believed God was truly speaking with his people — written by human beings, but actually inspired by God. On the road to Emmaus, Jesus now goes through 'all the Scriptures', explaining how they spoke of his own 'suffering' and 'glory'. Later, back in Jerusalem with his followers, he does the same: going through 'the Law of Moses, the writings of the prophets, and the Psalms', he 'opened their minds to understand the Scriptures'. And the result of this extended Bible study, led by the Risen Jesus, is that the disciples find their hearts burning with excitement. The Scriptures, expounded by Jesus, bring sheer and utter delight.

The Risen Jesus is giving us here a vital clue about what it will mean to be his followers once he has departed. *Scripture will be central.* So the fourth building-block in following Jesus is to learn about him through the Scriptures and to give to the Bible the importance which Jesus himself gave to it. Those who love Jesus should love his Scriptures.

Ever since, Jesus' followers have found the Bible to be a source of endless encouragement. Here they have found promises to claim, truths to ponder, examples to heed and prayers to repeat. Here we find the whole counsel of God, which enlarges our minds; here we find food that nourishes and sustains our hearts. So let us feed on his Scriptures.

> *The Scriptures, expounded by Jesus, bring sheer and utter delight.*

A surprising lesson

Jesus wants us to make use of this amazing, God-given resource. Yet his insistence on this here in Luke 24 is all the more remarkable for three slightly different reasons:

1. The Scriptures are important, even though we now have the Risen Jesus

Conceivably, Jesus could have said something like this: "Now I am back from the dead, you have something far more exciting to focus on than an old book!" Yet he says no such thing. The resurrection is indeed life-changing, but the Bible is not thereby rendered redundant. If anything, we need it all the more – both to learn how Jesus' coming fits into the Old Testament, but also to help us in our ongoing relationship with the Risen Jesus.

Sadly, we can easily go wrong at this point. We come to know Jesus, but sometimes we then think that we have an independent 'hotline' to God which does not need the guidance of the Scriptures. "Who needs the Bible and its difficult words, when you've got direct access to Jesus himself?" The danger, however, is that we then start following an imaginary Jesus, suited to our own likings.

Some people start following a 'gentle Jesus, meek and mild', who never speaks out strongly against sin. Others follow a Jesus who (not surprisingly) ends up endorsing all their own prejudices and agendas. Either way, Jesus becomes merely a pale reflection of our own preferences. Instead of following Jesus, it's we who now are taking the lead; we start making Jesus in *our* image! To avoid all this, what we need is to be following the authentic, awesome Jesus revealed to us in the Bible.

In other words, we need the Scriptures to keep us on the straight and narrow, because the Scriptures alone reliably teach us about Jesus as he really is. Effectively, Jesus is saying something like this: "You need me, but you also need the Scriptures. I am the truth, but they are too. Follow *me* by submitting to *them*."

> The Scriptures alone reliably teach us about Jesus as he really is.

2. The Scriptures are important, even though we now have the Holy Spirit

This too might come as a surprise. The Risen Jesus has been promising his disciples the gift of his Spirit (as seen in chapter 3); yet he insists it does not make the Bible unnecessary. The Risen Jesus knows such thinking may lead us down a false track – not because the Holy Spirit will mislead us, but because we ourselves may misinterpret what the Spirit is saying. Here again, without the guiding control of the Scriptures our sinful hearts may begin to follow our own desires.

So, before returning to his Father, Jesus makes clear that he is leaving not just the gift of his Spirit but also the equally precious gift of the Scriptures. Yes, the one might be coming to Jesus' followers in a sudden new way at Pentecost, whilst the other had taken centuries to produce; even so, *both* the receiving of God's Spirit *and* the reading of the written Scriptures are vitally important for God's people. They must not be played off against one another. Again, the one may bring us an experience of God's love into our hearts, the other a knowledge of God's truth to our minds, but wise followers of Jesus will relish both. In other words, those who truly love God's Spirit will love God's Word, and those who truly love his Word will love his Spirit.

3. The Scriptures are important, precisely because of the example of the Risen Jesus

Note Jesus' own remarkable attitude towards the Bible's truth and authority. Jesus here demonstrates how his whole ministry had been *fashioned by the Scriptures*. In going to the cross, he had been inspired by prophecies and patterns found in the Bible: the Scriptures had been his own hope and these he had now fulfilled. Jesus was truly a man *under the authority of Scripture*.

If this was true of the Risen Lord, how much more should it be true of us? What was true for Jesus should now be equally true for Jesus' followers.

In the light of Luke 24, therefore, we are presented by Jesus with some key questions:

- Do we love the Bible? If we value the resurrection, the cross and the Spirit, do we also value the Scriptures?
- Do we ever elevate our own experience (of Jesus or the Spirit) above the Bible? Or will we always test it against the teaching of Scripture?
- As Jesus' followers, will we follow Jesus' example and submit ourselves to the Bible's authority? Will we seek to believe its truth and obey its commands?

Scripture according to Jesus

In chapter 9 we will focus in more detail on how we can obey the teaching of Scripture, but for now we need to examine our attitude to Scripture itself. What *is* the Bible? Why should we give it this pivotal importance? Why does it have such authority? Put more technically, what should be our 'doctrine of Scripture'? As already indicated, a vital clue here will be to observe the attitude of Jesus.

Box 4a – The God who speaks his Word:
Old and New Testament references

THE PSALMISTS PRAISE GOD FOR HIS REVELATION

Our God is in heaven;
he does whatever he wishes.
The gods of other nations are made of silver and gold,
formed by human hands.
They have mouths, but cannot speak,
and eyes, but cannot see.

PSALM 115:3–5

The laws of the LORD are right,
*   and those who obey them are happy.*
The commands of the LORD are just
*   and give understanding to the mind ...*
They are more desirable than the finest gold;
*   they are sweeter than the purest honey.*
They give knowledge to me, your servant;
*   I am rewarded for obeying them.*

PSALM 19:8, 10–11

Your word, O LORD, will last for ever;
*   it is eternal in heaven. ...*
How I love your law!
*   I think about it all day long. ...*
How sweet is the taste of your instructions –
*   sweeter even than honey! ...*
Your word is a lamp to guide me
*   and a light for my path. ...*
The heart of your law is truth,
*   and all your righteous judgments are eternal.*

PSALM 119:89, 97, 103, 105, 160

GOD'S WORD THROUGH THE PROPHETS

As high as the heavens are above the earth,
*   so high are my ways and thoughts above yours. ...*
So also will be the word that I speak –
*   it will not fail to do what I plan for it;*
*   it will do everything I send it to do.*

ISAIAH 55:9, 11

I am pleased with those who are humble and repentant,
*   who fear me and obey me.*

ISAIAH 66:2

My message is like a fire,
*   and like a hammer that breaks rocks in pieces.*

JEREMIAH 23:29

PETER AND PAUL'S APPROACH TO THE OLD TESTAMENT

No one can explain by himself or herself a prophecy in the Scriptures. For no prophetic message ever came just from human will, but people were under the control of the Holy Spirit as they spoke the message that came from God.

2 PETER 1:20–21

The Holy Scriptures ... are able to give you the wisdom that leads to salvation through faith in Christ Jesus. ...

All Scripture is inspired by God ... and is useful for teaching the truth, rebuking error, correcting faults, and giving instruction for right living, so that the person who serves God may be fully qualified and equipped to do every kind of good deed.

2 TIMOTHY 3:15–17

Approaching the Old Testament

First, we should note how Jesus here is in overall agreement with his fellow Jews on this matter. The people of Israel (as seen from Box 4a) had developed a keen understanding of God's Word. They accepted their responsibility to treasure this divine Word and preserve what had been given to them. Even though sometimes this Word had revealed their disobedience and judged them, yet strangely they still preserved it – precisely because this was a Word which they had not invented for their own comfort but which they sensed they had received from their holy God through his servants.

Jesus himself clearly agreed with this approach. We never see him denouncing this attitude or trying to distance himself from it in some way. Instead there is every indication that Jesus was a person saturated with Scripture, deeply influenced by its prophecies and prayers, keen to explain and defend its teaching, ready to submit to its rules. This submissive approach to Scripture (already noted in Luke 24) is seen elsewhere throughout Jesus' life. Here are some examples from the other three gospels:

Matthew's gospel

- Jesus makes clear this fundamental priority within his ministry when facing temptation by the Evil One. Three times, he answers Satan with these solemn words: "The Scripture says ..." (4:4, 5, 10).
- In the Sermon on the Mount he asserts categorically that he has "not come to do away with" the Old Testament laws, but rather to "make their teachings come true" (5:17).
- Later in Jerusalem he chides some of his critics with these words:

> *"You don't know the Scriptures or God's power."*
>
> MATTHEW 22:29

In keeping with this, Matthew himself points out on numerous occasions how events in Jesus' life took place 'in order to make what the LORD had said through the [Old Testament] prophet come true' (1:22–23, 2:15, 17, 23).

Mark's gospel

- When debating with opponents, Jesus quotes some of God's words through the prophet Isaiah ("It is no use for them to worship me, because they teach human rules as though they were God's laws!") and then warns: "You put aside God's command. ... In this way the teaching you pass on to others cancels out the word of God" (7:7–8, 13).

John's gospel

- Despite claiming himself to be the embodiment of all truth ("I am ... the truth": 14:6), Jesus also asserts the truth of Scripture: "what the scripture says is true for ever" (10:35). In praying to God, he simply says,

> *"Your word is truth."*
>
> JOHN 17:17

- In making the point that merely studying Scripture may be futile (if conducted without faith in him), Jesus boldly asserts that Scripture's power lies in its capacity to speak truly about *him*: "These very Scriptures speak about me" (5:39).

From such comments, we can deduce this startling paradox: Jesus was himself both *subject to* Scripture and simultaneously the *subject-matter of* Scripture. He both obeyed the Scriptures within his own life and believed that they spoke about him. That's why in Luke 24 he showed how his ministry had fitted into Scripture's teaching and also pointed out in all the Scriptures 'the things concerning himself'. Put another way, although in some senses he was the *Lord of the Word*, he did not cease to be the *Servant of the Word*. He did not use his own unique authority to demean the Scriptures but rather bequeathed on them his own authority.

This cuts out, at a stroke, the very common idea that we can somehow follow Jesus without also following Scripture, that we can somehow use our elevation of him as a means of down-playing Scripture. To love Jesus is to love the Word – the Word which Jesus himself loved, lived by and died by, the Word, which he publicly reaffirmed in his teaching, death and resurrection.

No wonder, then, that the New Testament writers follow Jesus with this high regard for the Hebrew Scriptures (see Box 4a again): they saw them as coming from God with unique authority, seeing all Scripture as 'inspired' by God (or, more truly, 'God-breathed'). Behind the human authors of Scripture, they affirmed, was the work of God the Holy Spirit. If the Bible was a human book, it was also a divine book.

What the Scriptures said, God said.

This then explains how the apostles could slip interchangeably from saying 'Scripture says...' to saying 'God says...' (Galatians 3:8, 22; Romans 4:3; 9:17; 10:19–21). The two amounted to the same thing: what the Scriptures said, God said. These Scriptures were therefore to be received as the 'very words of God' (Romans 3:2).

It also explains why one of the apostles' key aims in speaking of Jesus was precisely to show how the story of Jesus was the true fulfilment of this longer biblical story. Thus for them, Jesus' coming did not deny Scripture's truth but only affirmed it all the more. The activity and actions of God, which they had witnessed so powerfully for themselves in Jesus, only confirmed that the same God had truly been active in the past (as revealed in the Scriptures). Indeed, truly, *his story* (Jesus' life, death and resurrection) was the climax of all *history* (God's story in the Bible).

Approaching the New Testament

If this is how Jesus and the apostles viewed the Old Testament, then there is a strong argument that this should also be the way we approach the New Testament – the Scriptures left for us by Jesus and the apostles themselves.

Because the apostles saw the Jesus-event as the true fulfilment of the Old Testament story, they would quickly have seen their own writings (which alone describe and explain that Jesus-event) as a necessary 'sequel' within the Scriptures – a second part in God's unfolding drama. Their writings would soon be seen as being on an equal footing with the Old Testament.

This self-consciousness amongst the apostles (that they were the conveyors of further Scripture) can be seen in several places. Peter cites Paul's words as 'Scripture' (2 Peter 3:16) and Paul claims an authority to speak from God (Galatians 1:1; Romans 1:1). Almost certainly, this came about precisely because they were given this role and function *by Jesus himself*. Since Jesus knew he would never write anything himself, he instead gave this task to his apostles, sending them out on his behalf to act as his special messengers. Effectively, they were commissioned by him to give a truly authoritative account of his life (as it were, as his authorised biographers). They would also be given Jesus' authority to augment his teaching – that is, to draw out the true implications of his coming for those who would respond to the Good News about him. Believers have always needed to know not only the *words* of Jesus (what he said) but also the *works* of Jesus (what his coming achieved).

We see this process, this commissioning of the apostles, both in the way in which Jesus first called them (Mark 3:13–15) and also in the way he later describes them shortly before his departure as his appointed 'witnesses' (Matthew 28:16–20, Luke 24:48; Acts 1:8; 10:42). Jesus' apostles were entrusted by him to speak of him truly and authoritatively.

More than that, Jesus gave them an express promise:

*"I have much more to tell you, but now it would be too much for you to bear. When, however, the Spirit comes, who reveals the truth about God, **he will lead you into all the truth**. He will not speak on his own authority, but he will speak of what he hears, and will tell you of things to come."*

JOHN 16:12–13

The apostles are promised that the Spirit will guide them to speak Jesus' truth to Jesus' people. First, they will not forget anything of importance spoken by Jesus. Secondly, they will be taught any further things that are necessary – those things (the "much more") that Jesus had not been able to say during his lifetime.

It therefore becomes a promise to us, not that we will be led into new truth beyond that given to the apostles (which is not necessary), but rather that what the apostles taught in his name is indeed true and comes authoritatively from Jesus by means of his Spirit. The New Testament is therefore the commissioned deposit of Jesus' truth for his followers. As such, we are to receive it as from Jesus himself. It is his word to his people, trustworthy and reliable.

Indeed, looking at this from God's point of view, one can sense how this faithful account concerning Jesus was a necessary part and indeed a vital corollary of his sending Jesus in the first place. Why would Jesus have bothered to come – let alone to die – if all the people living in later times would find it virtually impossible to find out what he had done? God's great rescue operation would have been wasted – lost for all time. No, within the purposes of God, it was essential that there be an accurate account of Jesus' work.

> *The New Testament is therefore the commissioned deposit of Jesus' truth for his followers.*

That authoritative record, so Christians claim, is the New Testament. This means that, whilst the Old Testament truly prepares us for his coming *before* the event (as Jesus teaches in Luke 24), the New Testament truly describes that coming *after* the event. Thus both Old and New Testaments, when combined together, truly teach us about Jesus.

It is in this sense that we can access Jesus only through the Scriptures. Yes, as already noted, he meets us in his risen power by his Holy Spirit. Yet we would not know Jesus at all (or recognise that the person we were meeting truly *was* Jesus), if it were not for the account of him in the Bible. The Scriptures alone have the authority to tell us who he truly is and what his will is for us. Scripture is God's chosen gateway through which alone we must go, if we want to be confident that we are reaching the real Jesus.

In conclusion, then, a Christian approach to Scripture is ultimately rooted in the character of God himself.

- *God the Father is a speaking God*: he is well able to speak to us, his creatures, and longs to be in relationship with us – revealing himself to us and also his perfect will for us.
- *Jesus, God's Son, submits to Scripture*: although he is the Lord of the Word with authority *over* it, he yet places himself *under* it, giving us an example to follow.
- *The Holy Spirit is the One who inspires*: he was able to work in (or, better, 'breathe upon') the biblical writers in both Old and New Testaments, leading them into all those truths which God wished for us to know.

A non-believer, who denied these great truths about God, might well see the Bible as no different from any other book. Those who believe in this God, however, have these three good reasons (and more) for seeing it quite differently. If we wish to be Jesus' followers, we should follow his example, giving our allegiance to Scripture for his sake and looking to it as God's revealed Word brought to us by his Spirit.

> *Scripture is God's chosen gateway through which alone we must go, if we want to be confident that we are reaching the real Jesus.*

Living under Scripture

So Jesus' followers should have a humble attitude towards the Bible. As God said to Israel, so Jesus says to us:

> "Human beings cannot live on bread alone but need every word that God speaks."
>
> MATTHEW 4:4 (BASED ON DEUTERONOMY 8:3)

God's word is to be treasured as our staple diet. Jesus' own teaching gives us some pictures here:

The seed

In his parable of the sower (Mark 4:1–20), Jesus teaches us that we are like fields receiving the 'seed' of God's word. He is asking us: what kind of soil are we? As God's word goes out, what response will it receive? Will we let other concerns in our lives 'choke' its message like weeds, so that we become unfruitful soil? Or will we receive the 'seed' humbly so that it grows well?

The vine

Jesus pictures himself as a vine (John 15:5–8): "I am the vine, and you are the branches." Again, he is looking for followers who 'bear much fruit' but warns that this only happens when people 'remain' in him: if we start living without him, he may need to prune us. The secret of a fruitful life, instead, is this: "remain in me" and let "*my words* remain in you".

Picking up these images, the apostles write very similar commands: 'Submit to God and accept the word that he plants in your hearts' (James 1.21). 'Christ's message in all its richness must live in your hearts' (Paul in Colossians 3:16). We are to live under Scripture and also to have its words living within us.

So, as Jesus' followers, we should commit ourselves to read the Bible (or to listen to it) whenever we can. And we should commit ourselves in advance to believe and obey anything that it clearly teaches:

- Where it contains warnings, we will heed them.
- Where it contains promises, we will claim them.
- When it teaches us spiritual doctrines (even about things we have not seen or yet experienced), we will trust them.
- When it contains clear commands, we will obey them.

This last point is of vital importance. Jesus is not looking for mere *biblical knowledge* but for *biblical obedience*, bringing our minds and our wills under the Bible's rule. The Bible is a very earthy book. Although it contains so much food for thought, its purpose is always practical too. It wants us not only to think about the truth, but actually to 'do ... the truth' (a strange phrase coined in 1 John 1:6):

Do not deceive yourselves by just listening to the word; instead, put it into practice.

JAMES 1:22

The Bible, however, is a vast book and, even for those who come to it with an obedient attitude, there are numerous difficulties to face. In this task, Jesus is well able, as it were, to take us by the hand and guide us in our understanding. Just as he helped those two disciples on the Emmaus road, 'opening their minds to understand the Scriptures', so he can help us today, if only we will ask for his guidance. Jesus is well able to lead us into his own truth!

> Jesus is well able to lead us into his own truth!

As we close this chapter, it may be useful to highlight some vital tips for Bible readers to ensure we approach the task with the right frame of mind.

1. We may have an open Bible, but that does not mean we fully understand it

In other fields of human learning we do not fully grasp everything straight away. The same is true here, as we begin this unique, spiritual type of learning. So, although Jesus is with us, we will always remain learners (or 'disciples') in his school. Indeed the complexities and profundity within the Bible may sometimes be used by God to keep us humbly dependent on him. Our faith is always (as an ancient Christian called Augustine* once said) a 'faith seeking understanding'. We are not to get dispirited at this point – and certainly not to take up a posture of arrogance towards the text. Instead we may put our unsolved problems in a pending tray, trusting that, if necessary, God will one day help us understand some of these things better. Let's not abandon our belief in the Bible's trustworthiness, but rather dig into it more deeply.

2. We may have a complete (or 'finished') Bible, but that does not mean the Holy Spirit has stopped speaking

Christians believe that, within the Old and New Testaments, God has given all the revelation he intends to impart (this is sometimes referred to as the closed canon* of the Bible). The chief reason why Christians make this assertion (that the Bible is now complete) is that God has given us the fullest possible revelation of himself in Jesus. There is nothing better in the pipeline – no further revelation to be expected. If you like, the complete salvation (offered in Jesus) is matched by a complete revelation (found in Scripture).

Yet sometimes those who give this (proper) emphasis to the final authority of Scripture are misheard as implying that they do not believe in the ongoing work of the Holy Spirit. Did the Spirit somehow stop speaking when the Bible's last page was written? Of course not! The Holy Spirit is eternally active, and without his daily work in our lives we could never begin – let alone continue – the Christian life.

> The complete salvation (offered in Jesus) is matched by a complete revelation (found in Scripture).

Moreover, if we ask God for wisdom, God's Spirit may give to us, as individuals, guidance which is related to our particular situations (about what should we do or say). We see examples of this in the Bible itself (Acts 16:6–10) and Jesus expressly promises the help of the Spirit for those standing on trial for their faith (Mark 13:11). James positively encourages us to ask God for this kind of godly wisdom (James 1:5).

However, any such *prompting* by the Spirit for the benefit of the individual believer is qualitatively different from his *inspiring* of the Scriptures, for *in Scripture we see what the Spirit intended to give to all believers for all time*. It can thus be called 'general revelation' in contrast to merely 'particular revelation' (that is, words of guidance or encouragement made to individuals or churches throughout history). It is the Spirit's voice as found in the Scriptures which is authoritative throughout every generation.

Once this distinction is safe-guarded, then we are set free to seek the Spirit's voice for today. We will always do so, knowing that any such supposed speaking by the Spirit today must be tested against his normative and authoritative speaking in Scripture. We will thus let other believers evaluate our interpretation of what the Spirit is saying to us (as Paul counsels in 1 Corinthians 14:29; see also 1 John 4:1).

Another way of making a similar point is this: We may have the Holy Spirit, but that does not mean we are free to go beyond the Bible. Jesus' promise that his Spirit would lead his apostles into 'all the truth' (John 16:13, quoted above) is often mistakenly read as a promise that the Spirit will lead Jesus' followers today into some further 'truth', even if it goes *beyond* the Scriptures or even *against* them. This is nonsensical. If the Scriptures truly express – albeit it in human words – the very mind and will of the Spirit, then we can never claim the Spirit's support for something that is contrary to Scripture. The Holy Spirit will never contradict himself.

The Holy Spirit thus continues to speak and reveal himself to this day; yet this will never go either *beyond* or *against* the plain teaching he has already given in the Scriptures.

> The Holy Spirit will never contradict Scripture.

Instead, the Spirit's role is to bring the truths of Scripture ever more powerfully into the experience of each believer. Yes, he continues to 'lead [us] into all the truth', but this is *into all the truth of those Scriptures that he has already given*. All good Christian theology is therefore effectively an elucidation of *what is already in Scripture* (replaying the Bible's themes afresh in each generation), rather than somehow being a development *away from or beyond Scripture*.

This leading into truth by the Spirit is in itself no small miracle. After all, however long we may live, we will always be making fresh discoveries *within* Scripture, so there really is no need to go *beyond* it! The Bible at this point is rather like a long cylinder driven down deep into the earth, which has a finite circumference, but which is endlessly deep (see diagram overleaf). Using this analogy, one can sense how the Holy Spirit will not take us outside the 'circumference' of Scripture, but he will take us ever further into its inexhaustible depth.

This means that we must resist all our proud attempts to improve upon what we have received. Nor will we give our ultimate allegiance to other possible guides – however helpful they might be. These include my own experience of the Spirit, human reason, or even longstanding Christian tradition. If there are things that God has *not* revealed to us in the Bible, we should be content and must respect his judgement. Some find an Old Testament verse to be useful here:

> *There are some things that the LORD our God has kept secret;*
> *but he has revealed his Law, and we and our descendants*
> *are to obey it for ever.*
>
> DEUTERONOMY 29:29

In other words, trust God for what he has *not* revealed, and obey him in what he *has*.

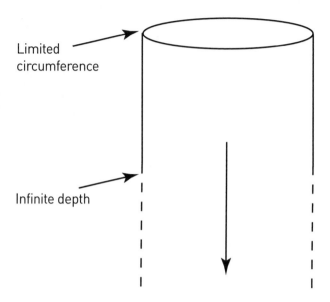

Limited circumference

Infinite depth

3. We may have the Bible and also the guidance of the Holy Spirit, but that does not mean we no longer need the help of others

Because the Bible is a complex book, we will always need to be learning from others. No single individual will ever grasp it all. In this sense, the Bible belongs to the church*, that is, to *all* God's people. So we need to learn from those who studied the Bible faithfully in the past (this is the proper place for valuing and respecting tradition). We also need to submit ourselves to learn from those who teach the Bible in our own day.

But someone might say, 'Who needs a human teacher, when we have a divine one – the Holy Spirit?' This attitude is both wrong and dangerous. Yes, as we have seen, the Holy Spirit can indeed speak to us personally through the Bible (see chapter 8). Yet 'teachers' are expressly listed as one of Christ's main gifts to the church (Ephesians 4:11), given to us precisely so that we might become mature in our thinking. Therefore, to ignore biblical teachers is not 'super-spiritual' but folly. Instead Paul urges: 'pay proper respect to those who ... instruct you in the Christian life' (1 Thessalonians 5:12). We should gladly place ourselves under the authority of those who teach us the

Scriptures; we should value any helpful commentaries on biblical books; and we should submit all our understanding of the Bible to the open scrutiny of others.

Conclusion

Believers in Jesus hang on his every word, given both in the gospels and through his apostles. We honour the inspired texts of the Old Testament, because Jesus did. And, most importantly, we always study the Scriptures, not for their own sake, but rather to grow in our love for Jesus (see John 5:39–40, quoted above).

Over the years, an organisation called Gideons International has placed over a billion Bibles in hotel rooms and other places. In the introduction to their Bibles, they describe the Bible in the following memorable way:

> It is supernatural in origin, eternal in duration, divine in authorship, infallible in authority, inexhaustible in meaning, universal in readership, unique in revelation, personal in applications and powerful in effect.

© THE GIDEONS INTERNATIONAL

Let's read the Bible as God's words to us. It is an incredible experience to hear the voice of the living God speaking to us, his people! So, the fourth building-block in the Christian life is to ensure we *feed ourselves on the Scriptures*. They are God's truth, and God's truth brings us his healing and grace, his wisdom and new life.

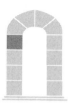

Building-block 4

Feed on His Scriptures – You Need God's Truth!

5

Participate in His Meal

They ... recognized the Lord when he broke the bread.

LUKE 24:35

For the next lesson in Jesus' 'master class' on that first Easter Day, we need to use our imaginations a little. Jesus drops a powerful hint, but we may miss it if we are not careful. It all has to do with the precise moment when God allows the Emmaus travellers at last to recognise Jesus. Note how this did not happen as they walked along the road. Instead, it was only when the Risen Jesus 'sat down to eat with them, took the bread and said the blessing; then *he broke bread* and gave it to them. Then their eyes were opened and they recognised him, but he disappeared from their sight'.

Luke then describes their dashing back to Jerusalem to explain to Jesus' other followers 'what had happened on the road, and how they had recognized the Lord...', he notes, '...*when he broke the bread*'. This is the punchline in Luke's story. He wants us to see something significant here, but what is it?

To get Luke's point, we would need to note how Luke speaks elsewhere in his writings about this 'breaking of bread' (see below). More importantly, we would need to remember how Jesus himself had already said and done some startling, even shocking, things at certain mealtimes earlier in his ministry (we shall look at the two most important ones in just a moment). There were several previous occasions when he had broken bread with his followers and had hinted that this action of breaking bread would somehow gain a whole new meaning for his followers.

So now, when Jesus was recognised in the breaking of bread, his followers would have begun to pick up some of this extra significance. They might sense that, through this moment of revelation, the Risen Jesus was effectively saying to them: "Those special mealtimes

I previously shared with you can now continue in a whole new way because I am alive again. Even if you cannot see me, I will be with you, and you will recognise my presence amongst you. And those puzzling words I said, when breaking bread, will now come into their own – you will now understand what I meant."

So there are hints here in Luke 24 that a fifth building-block for those who would be Jesus' followers is to be involved in a special meal of some kind, the meal that would soon be known as the 'Lord's Supper'. It sounds intriguing! We had better look now in more detail at what exactly Jesus had said at those earlier meals. Two such meals would have stood out in the minds of Jesus' followers – one in Galilee a year or two before, the other in Jerusalem just three days before. We will look first at the second meal, the most recent.

An earlier meal: the Last Supper

In Luke's gospel, much of Jesus' teaching takes place in the context of meals, when Jesus is enjoying what some call 'table fellowship' with a variety of people (see Luke chapters 7, 11, 14–15). In answering his critics, who noted the unsavoury and 'unclean' company he kept at such mealtimes, Jesus speaks about a God who goes out searching for the lost (Luke 15) and tells a parable about a great banquet to which the most unlikely people are welcomed (Luke 14:15–24). Picking up the well-known imagery of his day (which foresaw a great 'messianic' banquet to which God would invite all his faithful people), Jesus here is hinting that, as Messiah, he has the authority to host his own banquet and, like a good shepherd, to welcome in those whom he chooses. Indeed, one day, Jesus will host the greatest party of all! The writer of Revelation calls this the 'wedding feast of the Lamb' (Revelation 19:5–10). In the meantime, any meal hosted by Jesus will always be a foretaste of that heavenly banquet – open to all who put their faith in him.

These ideas form a powerful background to the meal which Jesus himself hosts once he has arrived in Jerusalem – a messianic banquet indeed, but with some startling differences. Gathered with his small company of followers in a discreet upper room, unnoticed by his enemies, Jesus shares what would be his last supper with his friends. Within a few hours, he would be betrayed to the authorities by one of his followers (Judas Iscariot) and, the next morning, he would be crucified outside the city walls. Not surprisingly, the events of that Thursday evening would be etched on his followers' memories for ever.

It was the season of Passover*. Each year at this time, the nation of Israel remembered God's great act of rescuing them from Egypt. They longed for God to rescue them again – this time from the Romans. That's why, as we read in Luke 24, Cleopas and his friend are depressed: "we had hoped", they say, that Jesus "was going to set Israel free" (Luke 24:21). Aware of all this, Jesus now hosted his own Passover meal. Yet, again, this would be a Passover meal with a difference. For, although it would look back to God's past deliverance, Jesus' Passover meal would look forward to a new kind of rescue. And, in the very centre of this whole story, Jesus would place... himself.

> *Jesus' Passover meal would look forward to a new kind of rescue.*

Within the Passover celebrations, there was always a 'breaking of bread' accompanied by a prayer, and also the drinking of some cups of wine, again with prayers and blessings. Suddenly, however, when Jesus gave his followers the bread, he dramatically changed the script. It was a one-liner, not easily forgotten, a sentence that put Jesus and his death right at the centre of human history. He said:

> "This is my body, which is given for you. Do this in memory of me."
>
> LUKE 22:19

Similarly, when he passed round the wine cup, there were these strange, almost macabre, words:

> "This cup is God's new covenant sealed with my blood, which is poured out for you."
>
> LUKE 22:20

Jesus was linking the bread and wine with his own body and blood – and expecting his followers then calmly to eat and drink them!

What could this mean? There are many things in these few short words, but Box 5a highlights some of the more important.

Box 5a – The meaning of Jesus' words at the Last Supper

- Jesus was making clear that his death was no accident (see above, chapter 2). He was talking about it quite openly; he was even *planning* it. His death, then, would be the result of his own active will (that's why he spoke of *giving* and *pouring out* his own body and blood).

- He wanted his followers to remember him in this particular way – not so much for his life and teaching, but rather for his death: "Do *this* in memory of me".

- He wanted to ensure that *each* of them ate and drank. Jesus' death was something which each person would need to thank him for individually: "given for *you*".

- He wanted them to repeat this meal, not just once, but again and again: "*Do* this" might be better translated as "*Keep on doing* this".

- He was clearly taking up the Passover imagery. Jesus himself would now be the true Passover Lamb (killed in our place, so that God's wrath and judgement could 'pass over' us). Jesus would therefore bring to God's people their freedom and rescue – rescue not from Egypt but from slavery to their own sin.

These few words of Jesus were indeed cataclysmic in their effect. Jesus was instituting a dramatic meal that would always remind his followers of his death – the place where Jesus died in our place. As Paul would later affirm, 'Christ, our Passover lamb, has been sacrificed for us' (1 Corinthians 5:7).

This then would explain the extra significance we sensed in Luke 24 when (just three days later) the Risen Jesus breaks bread in Emmaus. He is *signalling the importance of the meal which he had instituted only a few days earlier*; he is also saying that now, because of the resurrection, it will be possible for it to be a meal celebrated with joy and thanks.

Again we need to use our imaginations. If Jesus had remained dead, then perhaps his few followers would have got together occasionally (perhaps for an annual dinner?) in order to have a sad, depressing meal in memory of their dead hero. They would simply be doing what Jesus had commanded, but with heavy hearts and no clear idea as to what it was supposed to achieve.

Yet, that is precisely what did *not* happen! Ever since then, this meal has been celebrated around the world on a remarkably frequent basis. The only possible explanation for this is the resurrection. Only the resurrection could convert this macabre meal into a glorious celebration – of Jesus risen from the dead, of rescue now accomplished, and of sins now forgiven. And the signal that tells us the meal has changed from being something depressing to being a great delight is *that moment when Jesus broke bread at Emmaus.*

> *Only the resurrection could convert this macabre meal into a glorious celebration.*

The resurrection means we can obey Jesus' command without heavy hearts, remembering Jesus' death was not the end but rather our gateway into new life. Moreover, it also means that we can celebrate this meal in the presence of the Risen Lord himself. For Jesus is alive!

Another earlier meal: the 'feeding of the 5,000'

The other meal that was so significant in Jesus' ministry took place in Galilee one springtime, a few years earlier. Aware of its importance for Jesus' followers, all four gospel writers record this occasion, when Jesus fed at least 5,000 people from five loaves and two small fish (see e.g. Mark 6:30–44). This miraculous feeding was a clear demonstration of Jesus' spiritual authority and unique power over nature; it also showed his practical compassion for the hungry.

Yet John in his gospel (6:25–69) records some teaching of Jesus a few days later which gives this miraculous feeding a yet deeper meaning. Jesus begins by chiding his opponents for desiring only physical food; they should be seeking after "the food that lasts for eternal life" (verse 27). Then he reveals the startling truth:

> *"I am the bread of life."*
>
> JOHN 6:35

Jesus himself is God's gift of a food that will give eternal life. "Those who come to me," he continues, "will never be hungry; those who believe in me will never be thirsty." If people wish to have eternal life, being raised to life on the last day (verse 44), then "What God wants you to do is to believe in the one he sent" (verse 29).

Jesus goes further. What does it really mean to 'believe in the one he sent' (that is, in Jesus)? Are people just to believe that he was a great person sent by God? No, Jesus insists, they are to believe in him *as the one who came to die*, who gave his 'flesh' and 'blood'. So, continuing with the picture of faith as a kind of feeding on him, Jesus says:

> *"I am the living bread that came down from heaven. ... The bread that I will give ... is my flesh, which I give so that the world may live. ...*
>
> *I am telling you the truth: if you do not eat the flesh of the Son of Man and drink his blood, you will not have life in yourselves. Those who eat my flesh and drink my blood have eternal life, and I will raise them to life on the last day. For my flesh is the real food; my blood is the real drink."*
>
> JOHN 6: 51, 53–55

These words may have made little sense at the time. Indeed the imagery was so strong and violent that many – even amongst Jesus' own followers – were appalled (verse 60). After all, within Old Testament thought, it was wrong to eat any food with blood still in it. Yet here was Jesus seemingly encouraging his hearers to be cannibals!

Jesus, however, is using this graphic language to shock his followers into seeing this important truth: that we cannot be his followers if we do not come to him through his cross. His death for us must be the chief reason for our faith in him. We cannot just applaud him as a great teacher. He insists on being the one who died for us, whose death we need more than we truly know. So he demands that we must feed on him to the extent that we feed on his 'flesh' and his 'blood'.

> We cannot be his followers if we do not come to him through his cross.

Again (as with his words at the Last Supper), the death and resurrection of Jesus would in due course give a new understanding as to what Jesus had meant on this earlier occasion. Moreover, once his followers actually began to do what Jesus commanded – meeting in Jesus' name to break bread and drink wine – these words in John 6 would have been ringing in their ears with a whole new layer of meaning. Jesus' words here would alert them to the fact that they were not just holding a memorial service for their dead hero, nor indeed merely having a meal in the presence of their Risen Master. They were also, in some strange way, being invited to *feed on Jesus himself*, the very source of their life.

If we apply this to ourselves, then whenever we break bread in Jesus' name, we are to think of ourselves as in some way feeding on Jesus, receiving afresh his powerful life into our lives. The meal is therefore working on two levels. Outwardly, it is an ordinary meal with physical food which nourishes our bodies. On another (far more important) level, however, it is a spiritual meal with spiritual food, which nourishes our spirits. This is a great mystery – after all, we cannot actually *see* this spiritual feeding going on – but we should not doubt the power of this spiritual reality. Jesus is inviting us to a meal where he will feed us – with *himself*!

> Jesus is inviting us to a meal where he will feed us – with himself!

Yet there is a warning. None of this will happen if we are not exercising a real, personal faith in him. John 6 is an extended discourse on the need for faith – it is only "those who come to me" who "will never be hungry" (verse 35). There is no automatic magic in the bread and wine themselves. We cannot receive them without faith and expect them, by some mysterious means, *automatically* to give us eternal life. We can only *feed* on Jesus by exercising *faith* in him. If, however, we have put our faith in Jesus, then it is natural that we should want to come and be part of this meal. This is where we can feed on Jesus, and be nourished with the spiritual food that he gives us.

All this explains why, over the years, this meal has come to be called a 'sacrament'. In Christian thought, a 'sacrament' is a place of divine promise (technically a 'means of grace'), where *God promises actively to bless his people as they put their faith in him*. A sacrament is also an action that has an inner power and spiritual meaning which no one can see: outwardly, we look as though we are eating only bread, but truly and spiritually God is feeding our spirits with Jesus, the Bread of Life. Those who follow Jesus, therefore, will not want to miss out on this sacrament. It is the unique spiritual meal given to us by the Risen Jesus himself.

Key questions about the Lord's Supper

It is for all these reasons that we see the first Christians so frequently breaking bread together. In Acts, we will read of them 'breaking bread in their homes' (Acts 2:42) and of the believers gathering together in one place 'on the first day of the week to break bread' (20:7). Some of these first meals in Jerusalem may have been ordinary meals. Very soon, however, as the message of Jesus as Lord spread further afield, the pattern developed of celebrating this meal in a special way on a Sunday (the day of his resurrection) – *the Lord's Supper on the Lord's Day*. Ever since, churches have followed this pattern, some having a Sunday communion* service (or eucharist*) each week, others at least once a month. Was ever a command so obeyed? For Jesus' meal has been celebrated literally thousands and thousands of times since that first Passover meal in Jerusalem.

Box 5b

Was ever another command so obeyed? For century after century, spreading slowly to every continent and country and among every race on earth, this action has been done, in every conceivable human circumstance, for every conceivable human need from infancy and before it to extreme old age and after it, from the pinnacles of earthly greatness to the refuge of fugitives in the caves and dens of the earth.

GREGORY DIX, *THE SHAPE OF THE LITURGY* (1945)

We may still have some important questions here. For example:

Who can join in this meal? Is it totally open to all?

And *how* should we prepare ourselves for it? Are there any things we should avoid or approaches that are unhelpful?

On the first question, the Bible is clear that the meal is intended as a distinctive meal for Jesus' followers. On the one hand, we have seen Jesus' open policy of table fellowship with surprising people (including those termed 'sinners' in his day); this clearly demonstrates that his welcome extends to all people, regardless of where they are coming from. On the other hand, we also saw Jesus' insistence in John 6 that faith in him was essential; in his own graphic terminology, there would be no point in people eating the 'flesh' of Jesus if they did not have the faith in his death which Jesus was speaking about when he used that very phrase.

In the light of this, the first Christians soon established the simple rule that those attending this meal must first have been baptised. From earliest times, baptism with water and in the name of the Trinity* has been the sign of entrance into the Christian family (see Appendix C). It makes sense to keep this 'family meal' *within the family*. Another way of saying the same thing (since baptism is also seen as a sacrament given by the Lord to his people) is to observe that *only those who have received the sacrament of baptism should go on to receive the sacrament of communion*. This makes eminent sense. (It is worth noting that those churches which practise 'infant baptism' normally require people, once they are adults, to go through a further ceremony, known as confirmation*, in which they effectively reconfirm their baptismal vows and express their own faith in Jesus). Any believer in Jesus, therefore, who has been baptised and has publicly expressed their faith in Jesus, is welcome to start participating in this meal. And, thereafter, they should come to it, *on each occasion*, with an active and repentant faith in Jesus.

> The first Christians soon established the simple rule that those attending this meal must first have been baptised.

This is also clear from Paul's teaching in 1 Corinthians 10–11, where Paul emphasises the importance of people coming to this meal with active faith. Paul's extended teaching here also helps us answer our second question: how should we receive this sacrament? Paul is looking for a repentant spirit and is concerned at what he detects instead in the believers – their arrogance. In fact, the Corinthians were behaving in quite inappropriate ways (for example, some were getting drunk; others were not sharing their food with poorer people). Paul speaks out strongly against this disorder, stressing that we are all equals in Christ and must not put each other to shame (1 Corinthians 11:22).

It is important to note some of his other teaching here:

My dear friends, keep away from the worship of idols. ... The cup we use in the Lord's supper ... when we drink from it, we are sharing in the blood of Christ. And the bread we break: when we eat it, we are sharing in the body of Christ. Because there is the one loaf of bread, all of us, though many, are one body, for we all share the same loaf. ...

You cannot drink from the Lord's cup and also from the cup of demons; you cannot eat at the Lord's table and also at the table of demons. Do we want to make the Lord jealous?

1 CORINTHIANS 10:14, 16–17, 21–22

After reminding them of the words Jesus had used at his Last Supper in Jerusalem, Paul then continues:

Every time you eat this bread and drink from this cup you proclaim the Lord's death until he comes. It follows that if anyone eats the Lord's bread or drinks from his cup in a way that dishonours him, he or she is guilty of sin against the Lord's body and blood. So you should all examine yourselves first, and then eat the bread and drink from the cup. For if people do not recognize the meaning of the Lord's body when they eat the bread and drink from the cup, they bring judgement on themselves as they eat and drink.

1 CORINTHIANS 11:26–29

From this, we can draw out the following guidelines for how we ourselves should receive the Lord's Supper:

1. We should all examine our lives carefully

This is Jesus' meal for sinners who want to be cleansed and forgiven through his cross. It is not for people who hope they can be forgiven without turning from their sins, or who do not recognise 'the Lord's body' – Jesus' body broken on the cross for them. Since communion* services should always include an act of confession*, in which we ask God for forgiveness, we should ensure we do this sincerely. Otherwise, we 'bring judgement' on ourselves.

2. We should be aware of the Lord's presence

We do not treat this meal lightly. There is a real 'sharing' in the body and blood of Christ. Even if this is hard to define more exactly, the Lord Jesus is present by his Holy Spirit and he is opposed to anything in our lives that stands against him. Though invisible, Jesus is effectively the true leader or 'host' at this meal; we are meeting, not just in his name, but actually *in his presence*.

3. We should note that true believers are all part of Christ's 'body'

We are all sharing in the same bread; none of us is more important than any other – the ground is equal at the foot of the cross. So we should be united, showing peace, love and forgiveness to each other. In his teaching, Jesus had emphasised the importance of making peace with our brothers and sisters* before proceeding with our worship of God (Matthew 5:23–24). So we need to take this issue very seriously when we come to this act of worship. Furthermore, Paul teaches here that we are all now members of Christ's spiritual 'body' (1 Corinthians 10:17; 12:27). So we need, in this second sense too, to 'recognise the Lord's body' as we gather in his name. Each believer is valuable to Christ as a unique member of his body; we should therefore ourselves value each brother or sister 'for whom Christ died' (Romans 14:15).

So the fifth building-block in following Jesus is to *participate in this unique meal*, this sacrament of the Lord's Supper. At this point, we can look back and see how, after teaching first about his death and resurrection, the Risen Jesus in Luke 24 was then giving three further gifts to his followers: *his Spirit, the Scriptures and now this sacrament*. We are to value each gift in its own way.

Different Christian groups have sometimes emphasised one of these three above the others. This has led over the years to different 'streams' appearing in Christ's church (see p.192 in the epilogue). Partly, this may have come about because these three gifts deliberately touch us at three different points of our human personalities (namely, our spirits, our minds and hearts, our eyes and bodies). The Risen Jesus, however, clearly wanted us to enjoy each of them to the full, and for every part of our personalities to be touched by his grace.

With regard specifically to the sacrament of the Lord's Supper, this means we should never treat this meal flippantly. Instead we should see it as an opportunity to meet with the Lord, to enjoy his forgiveness and to be a visible part of his family. For this is the place where:

- We can come when we are broken and hurting, when we need God's forgiveness or feel unwanted or unworthy.
- We can tell again the great story of Jesus, proclaiming the truths of his resurrection, cross and Spirit (chapters 1 to 3 above).
- We should hear the Bible read and preached (chapter 4); indeed the story of the Scriptures comes alive at the Lord's Supper in a dramatic way, as we find ourselves joining in the action.
- We come together to share in a family meal, meeting with the Risen Jesus and feeding on him in a unique way.
- We are given a foretaste of the great banquet that Jesus is preparing for us in future.

Building-block 5

Participate in His Meal
– This is Your Spiritual Food!

Bear Witness to His Reign

"You are witnesses of these things."

LUKE 24:48

Jesus' final lesson on that first Easter Sunday was like a 'sting in the tail'. After unpacking these five aspects of the Good News, he made it plain to his followers that *they* now had a major task on their hands. The resurrection revealed that Jesus was God's appointed king: they now had to pass on this news to others and do all they could to extend the reach of his kingdom.

Luke helps us to imagine some of the feelings they would have gone through in that upper room (24:41): first, sheer disbelief and incredulity (could this really be Jesus here in their midst?), then joy and excitement (it was true!). But then what? Almost certainly, there came a dawning realisation of an awesome, even fearful, responsibility. For if this Good News of the resurrection was not just for them, but was for all people everywhere, then *who would be going out into the world with this message?* Would it be Jesus himself? No. As if reading their minds, Jesus spells it out plainly: "the message about repentance and the forgiveness of sins must be preached to all nations, beginning in Jerusalem. *You* are witnesses of these things" (verses 47–48).

Jesus is saying in effect, "This is the message the world has been waiting for, but it's not my job to tell the world – it's yours!" Or, if you like, "My mission has been accomplished. Yours is just beginning!" Indeed, in the parallel account of that first Easter day in the gospel of John, this is almost exactly what Jesus says: "As the Father sent me, so I send you" (John 20:21).

'Mission' means, literally, being 'sent out'. So from that moment onwards, Jesus' followers knew he was giving them a new mission in life. The joy of Easter and the task of mission would always go hand in hand. They could not have the one without the other.

This is a startling reality check. Jesus has performed the unique act of saving the world, but right now, the task of letting the world know about it lies in the hands of a tiny group of men and women in Jerusalem! What, if they are not up to it? Jesus has no other plans. His own work is done and he will soon be returning to his Father in heaven – in the event we refer to as his ascension*. The long-term success of his work is invested in those few followers he is leaving behind. What if they fail?

> The joy of Easter and the task of mission would always go hand in hand.

Those men and women in Jerusalem were thus left with a daunting responsibility. For Jesus' sake they had a job to do. *But so do we.* The message of Jesus' dying love for everyone cannot – must not – stop with us. Jesus is the king, and his kingdom needs to be proclaimed and implemented.

If this makes us suddenly feel quite small or afraid, Jesus goes on immediately to talk about the Holy Spirit (verse 49): "I myself will send upon you what my Father has promised. But you must wait in the city until the power from above comes down upon you."

God knows we cannot fulfil this task on our own, so he sends his Holy Spirit. Only the Spirit *of* Jesus can take this message *about* Jesus and convert it into a glorious reality – both in our own lives and in the lives of others. As we saw in chapter 3, only Jesus' Spirit can reveal and convey the reality of Jesus' lordship and rule. This means we are not left on our own with this task of mission; instead we have Jesus' outgoing Spirit to lead us, to guide us and empower us. Yes, the message about 'repentance and forgiveness' must be 'preached', but the Spirit will do the preaching through us.

> The message of Jesus' dying love for everyone cannot – must not – stop with us. Jesus is the king, and his kingdom needs to be proclaimed and implemented.

So the sixth building-block in following Jesus is to be involved in the mission of King Jesus. It is to let his Spirit guide us outwards – to speak in his name, to show acts of love and compassion which speak deeply of his heart for all, and to do all that we can to bring the world under his just and kindly rule. By our words and actions, we are to bear witness to others that Jesus is the world's true king; each of us has a part to play in this vital task.

Box 6a – Good news from Jerusalem: 'God is king!'

How wonderful it is to see
   a messenger coming across the mountains,
   bringing good news, the news of peace!
He announces victory and says to Zion,
   "Your God is king!"...
The LORD will use his holy power;
   he will save his people,
   and all the world will see it.

ISAIAH 52:7, 10

For forty days after his death Jesus appeared to them many times in ways that proved beyond doubt that he was alive. They saw him, and he talked with them about the Kingdom of God. ...
   "When the Holy Spirit comes upon you, you will be filled with power, and you will be witnesses for me in Jerusalem ... and to the ends of the earth."

ACTS 1:3, 8

In Isaiah 52, the prophet had had a vision of messengers running swiftly away from Jerusalem with good news – the good news that Israel's God was truly king. Now in the short period after his resurrection, Jesus teaches the apostles about how God has become king through him ('he talked with them about the *Kingdom of God*') and then sends them out as his messengers and witnesses. Using a different image, they are to be like trumpeters and 'heralds' – those who went ahead of ancient armies announcing that a victorious king was approaching. We too are meant to pick up this challenge, going out into the world, giving a clear signal, and proclaiming in word and deed the good news that there is a new victorious king. Are we ready to run with the message?

God's heart for all people

But is this right? Does God really want us to be proclaiming and building up Jesus' kingdom? A good way to answer our hesitations is to consider the theme of mission in the Bible as a whole. What is on God's heart? We soon discover that God's heart is indeed for all people, and he himself is a 'missionary God'.

We see this in the very first book of the Bible. When human beings turned away from God and fell into sin, God's solution to this universal problem was, strangely, to focus down onto one particular individual, Abram (Genesis 12:1–7). Yet this was not because God was not concerned with the whole world; rather it was his unique strategy to undo the sin that had contaminated it. Thus he gave his

> God's heart is indeed for all people, and he himself is a 'missionary God'.

chosen servant a new name: he was to be Abraham, which means the 'ancestor [literally, 'father'] of *many nations*' (Genesis 17:5). Through him, God was promising to 'bless all the nations' (Genesis 12:3). Right here, back in Genesis, God was showing his concern for all people – ultimately to bring them back to himself.

Thereafter, God chose to focus on the one nation of Israel (Abraham's descendants), for he needed to have one people on earth whom he could teach and who could show forth his values to the world. Nevertheless, his long-term goal throughout the subsequent centuries of the Old Testament was *always to bless the entire world*. Israel was to be a people who served God as 'priests' (i.e. showing forth God's character to the surrounding peoples) and brought his 'light to the nations' (Exodus 19:6; Isaiah 49:6). Israel's prophets too, in various ways, clearly predicted a time when non-Jews (the Gentiles*) would be brought into God's people – what was sometimes referred to as the ingathering* of the nations. What was not so clear was *when* God would do this and *how*.

The New Testament gives the answer: '*when the right time finally came*, God sent his own Son' (Galatians 4:4); this was precisely so that the 'blessing which God promised to Abraham might be given to the Gentiles' (Galatians 3:14). In other words, Jesus' coming from God into our world was the moment when God's ancient master plan (to bless all people) could at last come into effect. That's why the

> We are seeing here God's longstanding (indeed eternal!) agenda of love for his whole world.

Risen Jesus says in Luke 24 that the time has come for the Good News to go out to 'all nations' (verse 47). He is signalling the long-awaited moment when God's promise to Abraham can at last be fulfilled. We are seeing here God's longstanding (indeed eternal!) agenda of love for his whole world.

Note too how this message of God's heart for all people will have meant so much to the person who himself wrote down Luke 24, for Luke himself was a Gentile. Almost certainly he had for many years been a God-fearer* – one of those who hovered on the fringes of the synagogue, looking in respectfully but from outside the Jewish race. But then came this brilliant message about Jesus – the Jesus who had died for all people; and suddenly Luke knew that he could now become a member of God's people, just as he was! He did not need to undergo circumcision or become a Jew. He simply needed only to have repentant faith in Jesus, Israel's Messiah.

So in his gospel, Luke, not unnaturally, is determined to show how Jesus had been truly the Man for Others – the Messiah of Israel who had come to open the kingdom to *all*. Moreover, Jesus had not been obsessed with his own concerns, but rather had been motivated by love for others. He had mixed with everyone. So Luke portrays him as spending time with both rich and poor, with men and women, with Jews and Gentiles, with notorious sinners and Roman soldiers (see e.g. Luke 7 – 8). Even when being nailed to the cross in agony, we see Jesus' concern, not for himself, but rather for a thief being crucified alongside him – and even for those who were driving in the nails. "Forgive them, Father!" (Luke 23:34).

And it was not just Jesus' actions. Luke's selection of the *stories* Jesus told also reveal Jesus' heart for all people. Think of the story of the 'good Samaritan' (Samaritans were fierce enemies of the Jews: Luke 10:25–37); or the parable of the lost son who was welcomed back by his father (15:11–32); or how Jesus retold the Old Testament story about God healing Naaman, an army commander in charge of Israel's enemies, the Syrians (4:27). All these were deliberately designed by Jesus to shock his hearers into seeing *God's concern for all people*.

Not everyone liked this message, but Jesus was undeterred and insisted on reaching out to the most unlikely people. When making his final stop before going up to Jerusalem, Jesus went into the house of a hated tax collector, Zacchaeus. When this man repented, Jesus declared, "Salvation has come to this house today!" And then he added a vital comment, which for Luke summed up the very heart of Jesus' ministry:

"The Son of Man came to seek and to save the lost."

LUKE 19:9–10

For Luke, the Jesus who here welcomed Zacchaeus was the same Risen Jesus who later called his disciples to go out as his witnesses to all nations. Evidently, then, this Jesus has a heart for everyone. His goal is to save people who, without him, are lost.

So, Jesus has a missionary concern, and this truly reflects God's own agenda and passion. God has a deep heart for all people, as seen in two key New Testament verses:

> God loved the world so much that he gave his only Son, so that everyone who believes in him may not die but have eternal life.
>
> JOHN 3:16

> God our Saviour ... wants everyone to be saved and to come to know the truth.
>
> 1 TIMOTHY 2:3–4

God wants everyone to know him and to experience his love.

Jesus' mission through his followers

Jesus' mission can only go forward, however, if Jesus' followers themselves take it forward. That's why, earlier in his ministry, Jesus had sent his followers out on what we might call 'mission assignments'. He needed to train his followers in what it was like to go out in his name. Jesus' words on that occasion reveal how he saw people as being like a harvest in danger of going rotten through never being collected:

> There is a large harvest, but few workers to gather it in. Pray to the owner of the harvest that he will send out workers to gather in his harvest. Go! I am sending you like lambs among wolves.
>
> LUKE 10:2–3

Jesus has a strong passion for mission, for bringing people into his inclusive kingdom. And he wants his followers to share this passion too – to play their part in bringing in the harvest.

This is exactly what we see them doing after the resurrection. Luke's second book (The Acts of the Apostles) is all about Jesus' followers going out in his name to all people. They too now have a heart for the lost. They do not stay for long in Jerusalem, but go all around the world. Jesus had repeated his command that they should be his witnesses, testifying that he was the true Messiah of Israel and the ultimate ruler of the world; but now he specified that they would be bearing witness to him "in Jerusalem, in all Judea and Samaria, and to the *ends of the earth*" (Acts 1:8). And off they went.

The story told in Acts is an amazing one: truly these were thirty years that turned the world upside down! Yet Acts is written to encourage us to be witnesses too – to pass on the Good News of Jesus to others through our words and through our lives. We see the first Christians...

- speaking about Jesus in Jerusalem, around the Mediterranean and in Rome, being ready to witness to him before both Jewish and pagan rulers (see Acts chapters 4, 22, 24, 26);
- setting up local communities which cared radically for people in need (2:45; 4:32–37) and sending money to help those caught in a famine (11:28–30);
- talking to complete strangers (8:26–40), accepting invitations into people's homes (10:25ff), and going from house to house with the message that people must repent and have faith in Jesus (20:20–21);
- praying together for boldness (4:23–31) and then sending out some of their number on missionary assignments (13:1–3), who then establish small congregations in remote places and later report back on what has happened (14:23–27);
- proclaiming by whatever means possible that *Jesus* (not the Roman emperor or anyone else) was the world's true Lord: "These men have caused trouble everywhere ... saying that there is another king, whose name is Jesus" (Acts 17:6–7).

And this is only what Luke had time to report. There will have been thousands of personal conversations – in homes, in fields and on the streets – as ordinary believers simply 'gossiped the gospel' with their neighbours and friends. There will also have been many acts of kindness as ordinary Christians allowed Jesus' light to shine through them. This is how the church of Jesus grows. This is how the Good News spreads that Jesus is king.

Matthew, in his gospel, gives us two key statements from Jesus to guide his followers in this task of mission. How *do* we play a part in God's bringing in his kingdom?

The first statement encourages us that our actions can have a disproportionate and transforming effect on our surrounding culture:

> *"You are like salt for the whole human race. ... You are like light for the whole world. A city built on a hill cannot be hidden. No one lights a lamp and puts it under a bowl. ... In the same way your light must shine before people, so that they will see the good things you do and praise your Father in heaven."*
>
> MATTHEW 5:13–14, 16

Inspired by this vision, Christians through the centuries have got deeply involved in their societies: serving as politicians, encouraging social reform, improving medical conditions, influencing public policy, educating children, campaigning against slavery and so on. They have caught Jesus' vision of seeking to bring the values of God's kingdom into the here and now – in a way which pleases God and brings praise to his name. If you like, they have prayed, and then tried to implement, the key phrase in the Lord's Prayer: "may your will be done on earth as it is in heaven" (Matthew 6:10). Communities and neighbourhoods can be transformed if Jesus' followers commit themselves to such involvement – seeing biblical principles for human society and then working tirelessly to make them a reality. In many contexts, such *actions* may indeed *speak louder than words*.

Jesus' second statement, however, balances this, showing us that *words too* are vitally important – Jesus' followers need to be speaking about him and then teaching people how to walk in his ways.

> *"I have been given all authority in heaven and on earth. Go, then, to all peoples everywhere and make them my disciples; baptize them in the name of the Father, the Son, and the Holy Spirit, and teach them to obey everything I have commanded you. And I will be with you always, to the end of the age."*
>
> MATTHEW 28:18–20

The resurrection means that Jesus is God's appointed Lord and king over the world. People of all nations are to come under his reign and obey his teaching. His followers must themselves obey him, and then they must go out into the world in Jesus' name to help others into this place of obedience. In other words, they must both *live in the light* and also *pass that light onto others* – both through what they say and through what they do. And as they do this, they have Jesus' clear promise: "I will be with you!"

Hesitating to proclaim Jesus' reign — by word or deed

Some of us may find this exciting. But many of us feel quite weak at this point: "What can I do that would make a difference in society?" Or, "Who am I to speak of Jesus? I wouldn't know what to say!" "And, anyway, I'm not a good advert: I know some non-believers who live a better and more attractive life than I do!"

How *can* we bear witness to Jesus' reign?

Our hesitations are compounded — at least in many Western cultures — by our context. European society, for example, has been enormously influenced by Christian activists in the past, but now so many philanthropic ventures have been taken over by the state (e.g. education and healthcare) that the opportunities for Christians to make an appreciable difference can seem harder to find.

Europe's Christian legacy has also had the effect of making many people cynical about matters of faith: religion is branded as responsible for bigotry and violence; people who make truth-claims are dismissed as really just playing power-games. Many are also cynical about Jesus; they think they know what Christianity is (and imagine it was long ago discredited), but in fact, they don't. They are often reacting to a distorted stereotype. They think the Christian faith is...

- all about rules – but it's a relationship!
- about losing their freedom – when in fact Jesus offers them true freedom!
- suitable only for a certain kind of person – when in fact it's for everyone!
- a load of myths – when it's rooted in historical truth!

- tied to tradition and the ancient past – when in fact Jesus makes everything new!

Many people also give the appearance of living comfortable lives, seemingly undisturbed about spiritual or personal issues. In fact, of course, many of these same people are miserable and depressed, perhaps outwardly comfortable but inwardly lost – but that's the side of them that we don't see.

Meanwhile, others are indeed going through hard times. In the West they frequently blame God for this, becoming bitter. In the 'two-thirds' world, however, where people's suffering is often so much more acute, there is often, paradoxically, a real openness to hearing the Good News. But here too there are barriers: family and tribal commitments, the influence of other religious systems, and often the brute need to give time simply to survival in tough situations.

In these circumstances, all of us are tempted to withdraw. Why try to influence society for good in Christ's name? And why bother to tell others of Jesus? What if they don't think they need forgiveness or greater freedom? What if their suffering is much greater than mine? And (though we don't often admit this) what if this might cause *me* to suffer for my faith?

We find all kinds of reasons, many of them quite cogent. Despite Jesus' call to be 'like light for the whole world', we become brilliant at doing what he told us not to: hiding our light 'under a bowl'. He called us to be like salt, but too often our salt is left in the saltshaker! Jesus remains the king, nevertheless, and news of his reign needs to be proclaimed in whatever way is possible – challenging unjust authorities, helping those in need, and calling people to come under his rule. We must live out the truth and also speak out the truth. The Good News of Jesus' kingdom is indeed true. People may prefer following lies, but the Good News is God's truth for his world.

> *We must live out the truth and also speak out the truth.*

Moreover, this news about King Jesus also involves important warnings. There is a "road that is easy", warned Jesus, which truly leads "to hell" (Matthew 7:13). God's judgement is a fearful reality which can make people "cry and grind their teeth" (Matthew 8:12). Jesus is the king who can dismiss people from his presence and say to them those chilling words: "I never knew you. Get away from me, you wicked people!" (Matthew 7:21–23; see 25:31–46). Paul affirmed that 'all of us must appear before Christ, to be judged by him' (2 Corinthians 5:10).

So, even if we don't think it is, *sin is serious*; all rebellion against King Jesus will be treated as such. God has established Jesus as king of the world and eventually 'all will fall on their knees' before him (Philippians 2:11). People may think they are fine, but it isn't necessarily so. Our task, then, is to awaken people to these urgent spiritual realities. We may be unpopular, but truth is true.

Biblical encouragements to witness to Jesus

The rest of this chapter focuses on the issue which, for many of us, is the most difficult: how can we speak about Jesus' reign in a way that is effective and compelling? How do we share the Good News appropriately?

In John's gospel we are given two good examples which may help us to answer this question.

1. Sharing the Good News is pointing others to Jesus

This is what John the Baptist did (John 1:19–34). First, he was honest about his own limitations: "I am not good enough." Next, he told people to look instead at Jesus: "*There* is the Lamb of God, who takes the sin of the world!" Finally, he added his own personal testimony: "I have seen it and I tell you that he is the Son of God." Here are three simple ingredients: humility of style, a steady focus on Jesus as the unique Saviour, and all backed up by personal endorsement and commitment. Later, John compared himself to the best man at a wedding, whose purpose is not to draw attention to himself but rather to the bridegroom (Jesus):

> "He must become more important while I become less important."
>
> JOHN 3:27–30

Our task, then, is not to worry about ourselves (we will be far from perfect), but rather to point people to Jesus and *his* perfection.

2. Sharing the Good News is bringing people to Jesus

This is what we see in Simon Peter's brother, Andrew. As soon as Andrew heard about Jesus, he at once 'found his brother Simon and told him, "We have found the Messiah"... Then he took Simon to Jesus' (John 1:41–42). Later, in Jerusalem, we see Andrew doing this again. When some Greek visitors to the city told him they would like to see Jesus, Andrew simply informed Jesus – acting as the go-between. Andrew just loved making connections. Like him, our task is simply to help people get in touch with Jesus. We can make the introduction; let Jesus do the rest.

> *Our task is simply to help people get in touch with Jesus.*

The New Testament gives us some further helpful guidelines:

> *Be wise in the way you act toward those who are not believers, making good use of every opportunity you have. Your speech should always be pleasant and interesting [more literally, 'full of grace and seasoned with salt'] and you should know how to give the right answer to everyone.*
>
> PAUL'S WORDS IN COLOSSIANS 4:5–6

> *Have reverence for Christ in your hearts, and honour him as Lord. Be ready at all times to answer anyone who asks you to explain the hope you have in you, but do it with gentleness and respect. Keep your conscience clear ...*
>
> PETER'S WORDS IN 1 PETER 3:15–16

In these commands from Jesus' apostles we learn that we are:

- to be ready at all times — through maintaining an inner reverence for Christ and keeping a clear conscience, living lives that are worthy of him;
- to speak of our hope in Jesus – both now and for eternity;
- to be full of grace; since God's grace is what we are talking about, we should speak of Jesus with grace, with gentleness and respect;
- to be 'salty'; that is, we are to be close enough to people to have an effect and also to find creative ways of injecting the light of Jesus into any dark situations we encounter.

In all this, we will need to be prayerful, asking God to guide us to people in whom he is already at work. People cannot come to Jesus, says Jesus, "unless the Father draws them" (John 6:44), so we will be praying that God's Spirit will be doing his own, unique work of convicting people about Jesus' truth (see John 16:8–11). Also, of course, we will always seek to be sensitive towards people's needs. After all, spreading Good News does not require us to be rude, unkind or unloving. Ultimately, it's a matter of honestly speaking the truth – the truth about Jesus' reign and the truth that we are his followers. At one level, as someone has helpfully put it, it's all about 'one beggar telling another beggar where to find bread'.

> It's all about 'one beggar telling another beggar where to find bread'.

Finding the words

What kind of things should we actually say? Are there particular things we can be preparing right now so that we can indeed 'make the most of every opportunity?'

At one level, it's important not to be too worried here about developing set formulas or pat answers. Every person and every conversation is unique and we need to respond appropriately. Our goal is simply to live under the rule of Jesus, letting Jesus guide us. So, as we pray, can we discern what Jesus himself might have said or done in this situation? After all, Jesus promised his special help and inspiration for anyone seeking to witness to him:

> "Do not worry beforehand about what you are going to say;
> when the time comes, say whatever is then given to you. For
> the words you speak will not be yours; they will come from
> the Holy Spirit."
>
> MARK 13:11–12

On the other hand, there is no harm in becoming a little clearer in our own minds as to some key things to say. Reading some of the material in Appendices A and B might help clarify your own thinking about the faith and how to explain it to another person. Alternatively, you may be able to encourage your friends to read the Appendices for themselves – or other books that deal in greater depth with some of their concerns.

Yet what if someone suddenly asked us about our faith and there were only two minutes left for us to give a reply?

Here, it's worth getting familiar with a tried and tested summary of the gospel. The *Why Jesus?* booklets (associated with the *Alpha* course) helpfully summarise the gospel, focusing on what Jesus offers. The booklet associated with the *Christianity Explored* course focuses more on the cross and our need for forgiveness. *Two Ways to Live* (originating from Australia) develops the theme of this present chapter – that Jesus is king – and challenges people to recognise that they have placed themselves, not Jesus, on the throne of their lives. Alternatively, you may find helpful the 'gospel presentation' in Box 6b (overleaf), which presents Jesus' cross as being able to bridge the gap between humans and God. Whichever you use, it's worth having some Bible verses committed to memory, so that you can speak some of God's words, not merely your own. Remember: Scripture has a unique power.

Another way would be to develop your own summary based on what we covered above in chapters 1 to 3. If, as we have seen, the gospel centres upon Jesus (his resurrection, his cross and his Spirit), then we might want to say something along these lines:

- Through the resurrection, God has established Jesus as king and has revealed that he wants 'all people everywhere to turn away from their evil ways' and to 'come to know the truth' (Acts 17:30; 1 Timothy 2:4).
- On his cross Jesus 'carried our sins' (1 Peter 2:24) so that, if we repent, God can truly and completely forgive us.
- Eternal life can become ours when we commit ourselves to come under Jesus' rule and to follow him as our Risen Lord. When we do this, he enters into our lives by his Holy Spirit, in keeping with Jesus' promise that God would send us his Spirit – "you will not be left all alone" (John 14:18).

Whatever we say, however, the important thing is to be both genuine (speaking what is true to our own experience) and truthful (conveying God's truth from the Bible), always pointing not to ourselves but to Jesus. Remember too the power of personal testimony: people will often be deeply touched and made more open to the Good News if we share honestly with them some of our own experience of God's reality in our lives, and of his faithfulness. Also note that real, lasting change often comes about when people hear the Word of God (in Scripture) as it starts to address them directly.

Box 6b – A gospel presentation: the 'bridge' diagram

DIAGRAM 1

☐ Many recognise that, if God exists, there is a vast gap (or 'chasm') between God and Humanity: he is our Creator, we just his 'creatures'; he is also 'transcendent'—that is, quite distinct from us (Isaiah 40:10-31).

☐ He is also utterly holy— 'unable to look upon that which is evil' (Hab.1:13). Human beings, by contrast, are selfish and tainted by moral evil ('there is no one who is righteous': Rom. 3:10).

☐ As a result, the Bible teaches that our sinfulness effectively places a barrier between us and God (Isa. 59:2; see also Gen. 3:23). The gap between us is caused by our 'SIN'.

DIAGRAM 2

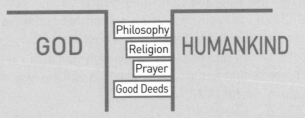

☐ Many people, being aware of this distance from God, try to reach out towards God, searching after him—hoping to find him or perhaps to earn his favour.

☐ Different people may try different tactics. Some will read books on religion or pursue 'philosophy' in some way. Others will try to do some of the things Jesus discussed in his Sermon on the Mount (Matt. 5-7), namely being:

    ☐ religiously observant,
    ☐ trying to pray in private,
    ☐ being good and kind to their neighbours.

- Yet there is a basic problem with each of these. However good in themselves, they do not get through to God—because none deal with the fundamental problem of human SIN. Put another way, they all fail because (as the diagram makes clear) they all start from humanity's side, not God's; none of them can reach to the other side.

- What is needed, then, is an initiative of God (something which starts from *God's* side of the diagram) and which deals with the fundamental cause of the gap.

DIAGRAM 3

GOD   HUMANKIND

- This is precisely what the cross is: it is offered by God as his solution to the problem of human sin and wrong-doing. 'God presented Jesus as a sacrifice of atonement' (Rom. 3:25). 'Salvation comes from the Lord' (Jonah 2:9), not from ourselves.

- On the cross, God 'made him who knew no sin to be sin, that through him we might be come the righteousness of God' (2 Cor. 5:21). Jesus effectively destroys the power of SIN by absorbing it onto himself.

- Again, Jesus the Righteous One 'died on behalf of the unrighteous in order to bring us to God' (1 Pet. 3:18). Through the cross Jesus is able thereby to remove SIN and then bring sinful human beings back across into the presence of God (we can have 'access' into God's presence: see Rom. 5:2; Eph. 2:18).

- A bridge has thus been established by Jesus' cross, which can bring us into God's presence and enable us to know him for ourselves.

The question is: have we walked across that bridge? To do so means simply:

a) acknowledging our need of the bridge (that we are sinful and need God's forgiveness)

b) thanking God for providing that bridge through the cross of Jesus, his Son.

In this way, we play our part in Jesus' great mission, first launched by him in that upper room when he commissioned his followers to go from Jerusalem to 'all nations'. Some of us may be better talkers and communicators than others. Some may have a particular gift of evangelism in their public speaking or in their friendships. Others, of course, may have a particular calling to spread the kingdom of Jesus through committed social action and practical concern. Each of these is a different gifting which Jesus uses to extend his kingdom. But all Jesus' followers are also commissioned with a message which we must be prepared to speak out – if (or indeed when) occasions present themselves.

That's why Peter told Jesus' followers to be 'ready at all times to answer anyone' (1 Peter 3:15). Are we ready? Jesus himself said, "Much is required from the person to whom much is given" (Luke 12:48). If we have been given the great Good News of Jesus, are we going to hoard it to ourselves, becoming like a stagnant pond? Or are we going to give it gladly away, so that others too might be refreshed? In the land of the Bible there are two inland lakes (Lake Galilee and the Dead Sea); the former gives all its water away and so remains fresh; the latter hoards everything it receives and so becomes 'dead' and putrid. Which one are we going to be like?

So the sixth and final building-block that the Risen Jesus gives to his followers is this: be actively involved in God's mission and *bear witness to his reign*. Jesus is God's appointed king and we must play our part, by word and deed, in extending his kingdom.

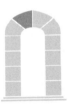

Building-block 6

Bear Witness to His Reign
– Others Too Need to Come under His Rule

PART 2

Learning from the Apostles

(Acts 2)

From Luke's Second Book:

The Acts of the Apostles
(chapter 2)

The Coming of the Holy Spirit (verses 1–8, 11–13)

When the day of Pentecost came, all the believers were gathered together in one place. Suddenly there was a noise from the sky which sounded like a strong wind blowing, and it filled the whole house where they were sitting. Then they saw what looked like tongues of fire which spread out and touched each person there. They were all filled with the Holy Spirit and began to talk in other languages, as the Spirit enabled them to speak.

There were Jews living in Jerusalem, religious people who had come from every country in the world. When they heard this noise, a large crowd gathered. They were all excited, because each one of them heard the believers speaking in his or her own language. In amazement and wonder they exclaimed, "These people who are talking like this are Galileans! How is it, then, that all of us hear them speaking in our own native languages? ... all of us hear them speaking in our own languages about the great things that God has done!" Amazed and confused, they kept asking each other, "What does this mean?"

But others made fun of the believers, saying, "These people are drunk!"

Peter's Message (verses 14–18, 21–28, 31–40)

Then Peter stood up with the other eleven apostles and in a loud voice began to speak to the crowd: "Fellow-Jews and all of you who live in Jerusalem, listen to me and let me tell you what this means. These people are not drunk, as you suppose; it is only nine o'clock in the morning. Instead, this is what the prophet Joel spoke about:

> 'This is what I will do in the last days, God says:
>   I will pour out my Spirit on everyone.
> Your sons and daughters will proclaim my message;
>   your young men will see visions,
>   and your old men will have dreams.
> Yes, even on my servants, both men and women,
>   I will pour out my Spirit in those days,
>   and they will proclaim my message. …
> Whoever calls out to the Lord for help will be saved.'

"Listen to these words, fellow-Israelites! Jesus of Nazareth was a man whose divine authority was clearly proven to you by all the miracles and wonders which God performed through him. You yourselves know this, for it happened here among you. In accordance with his own plan God had already decided that Jesus would be handed over to you; and you killed him by letting sinful men crucify him. But God raised him from death, setting him free from its power, because it was impossible that death should hold him prisoner. For David said about him:

> 'I saw the Lord before me at all times;
>   he is near me, and I will not be troubled.
> And so I am filled with gladness,
>   and my words are full of joy.
> And I, mortal though I am,
>   will rest assured in hope,
> because you will not abandon me in the world of the dead;
>   you will not allow your faithful servant to rot in the grave.

You have shown me the paths that lead to life,
and your presence will fill me with joy.' ...

"David saw what God was going to do in the future, and so he spoke about the resurrection of the Messiah when he said,

'He was not abandoned in the world of the dead;
his body did not rot in the grave.'

"God has raised this very Jesus from death, and we are all witnesses to this fact. He has been raised to the right-hand side of God, his Father, and has received from him the Holy Spirit, as he had promised. What you now see and hear is his gift that he has poured out on us. For it was not David who went up into heaven; rather he said,

'The Lord said to my Lord:
"Sit here at my right
until I put your enemies as a
footstool under your feet".'

"All the people of Israel, then, are to know for sure that this Jesus, whom you crucified, is the one that God has made Lord and Messiah!"

When the people heard this, they were deeply troubled and said to Peter and the other apostles, "What shall we do, brothers?"

Peter said to them, "Each one of you must turn away from your sins and be baptized in the name of Jesus Christ, so that your sins will be forgiven; and you will receive God's gift, the Holy Spirit. For God's promise was made to you and your children, and to all who are far away – all whom the Lord our God calls to himself."

Peter made his appeal to them and with many other words he urged them, saying, "Save yourselves from the punishment coming on this wicked people!"

Many of them believed his message and were baptized, and about 3,000 people were added to the group that day. They spent their time in learning from the apostles, taking part in the fellowship, and sharing in the fellowship meals and the prayers.

Life among the Believers (verses 41–47)

Many miracles and wonders were being done through the apostles, and everyone was filled with awe. All the believers continued together in close fellowship and shared their belongings with one another. They would sell their property and possessions, and distribute the money among all, according to what each one needed. Day after day they met as a group in the Temple, and they had their meals together in their homes, eating with glad and humble hearts, praising God, and enjoying the good will of all the people. And every day the Lord added to their group those who were being saved.

7

Share with Jesus' People

What happened next?

In part 1, we saw how Jesus on the first Easter Sunday gave his master plan for his followers. We are to focus on six main things: the resurrection and the cross; the Spirit and the Scriptures; a meal, and our mission in Jesus' name. Luke now picks up the story to show how his followers responded. Jesus had told them to wait in Jerusalem for something new: the Father's gift of the Spirit. In Acts 2 (see extracts above) we read the exciting account of what actually happened. Their Easter joy was followed by Pentecost power.

Acts chapter 2 is a great story — a true story of what God did. It was a unique event in the history of the world. Even though we are not to expect the Holy Spirit to do precisely the same for us (touching us with tongues of fire or helping us to speak in foreign languages), we can affirm that this truly happened on that one occasion, especially if we ourselves are those who know the Spirit's presence and power in our own lives. What God was doing here was marking the public launch of Jesus' new people, dramatically vindicating the message of Jesus, and so confirming his divine intention that we should be people who *honour his Son* and *welcome his Spirit*.

> *Their Easter joy was followed by Pentecost power.*

God gave to Peter an incredible boldness — the same Peter who, as described in Luke 22, had denied Jesus three times! Peter was thus enabled to launch that witness to King Jesus which Jesus himself had commanded. Here we see happening precisely what Jesus had predicted in Luke 24 (as we saw in chapter 6) – mission in

Jesus' name. In one sense, Jesus' mission had been accomplished, but in another sense his mission – that which he can inspire in and through his followers – was only now beginning.

Peter proclaims Jesus as *king*

Peter's words confirm the pattern of Jesus' teaching which we outlined in part 1 (especially chapters 1 to 3). Note how he focuses on:

- *The new life of Jesus' resurrection*. "God raised him from death," Peter says. Unlike great King David, "his body did not rot in the grave". Death could not hold him in its power. Indeed he was not only raised from the tomb, but had also now been exalted to the Father's 'right-hand side' – what is now known as his ascension. God had therefore vindicated him as the anointed king (the Messiah) and the Lord of the world. Peter witnesses to Jesus' unique identity, seen in both his resurrection and ascension.
- *The necessity of Jesus' death*. Even though some of his hearers had been involved with the events leading up to Jesus' crucifixion seven weeks before ('whom *you* crucified'), Peter does not tactfully omit the cross. Instead he boldly declares that this shameful, unlikely event had been in line with God's plan – his intention to rescue the world. When he then announces God's promise to forgive their sins and to rescue them from the coming punishment, there is an implicit connection to the cross, as the place where such punishment had been taken by Jesus, precisely to bring about forgiveness of sins (see Luke 24:47; Acts 20:28; and fuller discussion in chapter 2 above).
- *The new gift of the Holy Spirit*. In the Old Testament, the gift of the Spirit had been limited to certain people, but now this gift was being poured out (by King Jesus!) to *all* people: men and women, young and old, indeed to "all whom the Lord our God calls to himself".

Peter, as instructed by Jesus, is bearing witness to his reign. Note how he simply unpacks the same three great truths that Jesus himself had highlighted in Luke 24 (chapters 1 to 3 above). He then backs them up with frequent use of the Scriptures (e.g. Joel 2:28–32; Psalm 16:8–11), again as Jesus had strongly encouraged (chapter 4 above).

The result, perhaps not so surprisingly, is powerful. Peter's hearers, we read, were 'deeply troubled'. They may have sensed the horror of the cross. They may have been awestruck by the evident power of the Spirit. Or they may have pondered Peter's powerful application of the Scriptures, now fulfilled in the Risen Jesus. In particular, when Peter quoted Psalm 110 ("Sit here at my right until I put your enemies as a footstool under your feet"), they may have sensed the vital importance of not being one of the 'enemies' of this King Jesus – who had been so recently exalted by God to his throne in heaven.

Peter gave some straight commands to those who wanted to make a response: "Each one of you must turn away from your sins and be baptized in the name of Jesus Christ ... and you will receive God's gift, the Holy Spirit." Here was the punchline, the challenge flowing out from Peter's proclamation of Jesus as king. Many responded on that occasion and many have done so ever since (see chapter 1).

Jesus' followers respond: a vital model for us today

There is more to learn from Acts 2, however. In some important verses (41–47), Luke tells us what these new followers of Jesus did next.

In fact, these few verses will provide the basis for all we are going to be learning together here in part 2, as we learn from the apostles a further six building-blocks that are vital for those who want to walk in the ways of Jesus. In other words, by noting how the Holy Spirit guided Jesus' followers *then*, we will be guided as to how we should follow him *today*.

Verse 42 is the key verse. This is translated well in one version:

> *They devoted themselves to the apostles' teaching and to*
> *the fellowship, to the breaking of bread and to prayer.*
>
> ACTS 2:42 NIV

Here is a great model for Jesus' followers – a basic blueprint for the church's life for generations to come:

- apostles' teaching;
- fellowship*;
- breaking of bread;
- prayer.

It is an incredibly well-balanced programme, holding together different strands in the church's life that too easily fly apart: biblical teaching, practical concern for those in need, proper valuing of the Lord's Supper, and commitment to a life of prayer and worship.

The third bullet point is particularly intriguing. For it confirms what we saw (in chapter 5), that Jesus had given his followers this distinctive command to remember his death by 'breaking bread' together in his name. Here in Acts, we see them immediately putting this command into practice.

Yet the other three bullet points are fascinating too. From these, we will now in part 2 draw out six further themes that will help us to follow Jesus.

Here in chapter 7 we will focus on *the fellowship* (how we should share with our fellow believers). In chapter 8 we will focus on *prayer* (how we should worship God, both individually and corporately). Then, in the next four chapters, we will look at different aspects of *the apostles' teaching*: Chapter 9 will focus on what the apostles taught us to *believe* – their doctrines about Jesus and salvation. Chapter 10 focuses on what they taught us to *do* (or the kind of people we are to *become*) — their teaching about living the Christian life. Chapter 11 will focus on the apostles' challenge to *resist evil* – their lessons about Christian *warfare*. Finally, chapter 12 looks appropriately at what we are to *hope for* – what the apostles teach us about the *future*.

Let's look at each in turn to see what it means to truly walk, guided by the apostles' example, in the Jesus Way.

The fellowship of the Holy Spirit: practical sharing

'Fellowship'* is a strange word. What does it mean? We will discover that the very reason it is used so rarely outside Christian circles is precisely because it is trying to describe something unique within Christianity: the unique relationship that exists between believers because they all have something in common – the indwelling presence of Jesus' Spirit.

Peter's message was that those who followed Jesus would surely "receive God's gift, the Holy Spirit" (verse 38). This confirms what we said above (in chapter 3) that *every believer* has the Holy Spirit dwelling within them. Yet it also explains the great mystery of the church. For the church, unlike any other organisation in the world, is made up of people all of whom have the Spirit of their Master living within them! This means that there is automatically a connection between us. When we meet Christians for the first time, we already have something in common with them (or perhaps we should say, some*one* in common!). There is a love, a power, and a presence that draws us together: God's Holy Spirit.

This is what those first 3,000 believers discovered when they responded to Peter's preaching. They found that they shared together not just a common *faith* (in Jesus) but a common *life* (because of his Spirit within them and between them). The Bible then calls this reality 'the *fellowship* of the Holy Spirit' (2 Corinthians 13:13).

This fellowship is not just a spiritual reality; it should also translate into everyday reality and radical practice. The original Greek word (translated as 'fellowship') simply means that which is 'common or shared'. So fellowship means something like 'having or doing things in common' — exactly what we see those first believers putting into practice. Perhaps we will best get the sense of what fellowship means if we use instead the concept of *sharing* — a concept which sounds much more practical and earthy.

The church, unlike any other organisation in the world, is made up of people all of whom have the Spirit of their Master living within them!

So, after experiencing the Holy Spirit, the first believers immediately 'shared their belongings with one another' (verse 44). In fact, they decided to go so far as to 'sell their property and possessions, and distribute the money among all, according to what each one needed' (verse 45). This was real, practical sharing. What they now had in Jesus was worth far more than their possessions, so they gladly shared these with other believers who were in real need.

In the same way, our fellowship with other believers should not just be spiritual, but practical. We learn from later in Acts (4:32 – 5:11) that this initial response to the gospel did not require them literally to sell everything — there is not a total ban on possessions or personal wealth. Thus, as the New Testament develops, we see Christians using their money and possessions in different ways to build up their fellow believers (see e.g. 2 Corinthians 8 – 9). However, there remains here a strong biblical challenge, especially to Christians in the West. In what ways are we sharing our resources with our fellow Christians? We also need to hear this challenge whenever we think of the church

In what ways are we sharing our resources with our fellow Christians?

spread throughout the world. How are Jesus' followers showing their commitment to one another in practical and financial ways?

So the seventh building-block, as we follow Jesus, is to *share with Jesus' people*. This will mean sharing our care and our lives, showing our love in practical ways, and finding ways of expressing our strong commitment to one another. Every believer has the Holy Spirit dwelling within them. If each of us truly belongs to Jesus, we soon discover that, through him, we now belong to each other!

Jesus' new family: God's commitment to building his people

Some of us, however, may need help becoming convinced that this is part of what it means to be Jesus' followers: "Can I not follow Jesus without having to be so committed to his other followers?" If so, here are two insights from the Bible that can help strengthen our resolve. They come in the form of two questions: how would we respond?

1. Do we consider other believers as members of our new 'family'?

Jesus wants us to. On one occasion, when asked a question about his actual human family, Jesus looked around instead at those sitting near him and replied quite forcefully:

> "Who are my brothers? ... Look! Here are my mother and my brothers! Whoever does what God wants him to do is my brother, my sister, my mother."
>
> MARK 3:33–35

Jesus was establishing a new family – one that was centred on him, and obedient to God.

Family life can be painful for many; this may be because of difficult or broken relationships (sometimes leading to divorce), or because of personal setbacks or tragedy (fuelled in some parts of the world by the AIDS crisis or long-term wars). Even so, most of us recognise the great value of families. It is a horrible thing to be separated from one's family, to lose one's brothers or sisters, or to be orphaned.

Through Jesus, however, each believer has been brought into a new family: the church, the people of God, God's own family. After all, when we are born physically, we are inevitably born into a family (whether we like it or not!). The same is true when we are born spiritually. Jesus taught that believers are 'born again' through the work of God's Spirit upon them (John 3:3, 7). One consequence of this new birth is inevitably that we find ourselves in a new family.

> Some ... believed in him; so he gave them the right to become God's children.
>
> JOHN 1:12–13

This means that we are automatically in a family relationship with everyone else who, through Jesus, is also a child of God.

For most people, this is an exciting part of the Good News. As believers, we find we are no longer on our own. We belong. We have many new brothers and sisters, and God is our true Father (see chapters 2 and 3). If we have had difficulties in our human families, we now can experience something of what we have missed: the joy of being valued by others, and the delight of being deeply loved by God himself.

For others, however, there is a challenge here. They don't mind following Jesus on their own, but they don't want to share their lives with others. The saying goes, "You can choose your friends but not your family"; what if we find that we don't like those who are in this new family? Can't we opt out? No, we cannot have Jesus himself without also having Jesus' people! Jesus is forming a worldwide family, and his followers need to recognise that to belong to Jesus is to belong to his new people.

> **We cannot have Jesus himself without also having Jesus' people!**

Moreover, Jesus wants his family to be characterised by love – Jesus' unique kind of love:

> "And now I give you a new commandment: love one another. As I have loved you, so you also must love one another."
>
> JOHN 13:34–35

If so, then we must express this love, even if our fellow believers are people whom we do not naturally *like*. And we must do so in practical ways. For Jesus' sake, we are called to share with others in Jesus' family. This is something deeper than mere human *friend*ship; this is authentic, family-styled *fellow*ship.

2. Do we realise just how important it is to God himself that he builds a new people?

We are often so individualistic and wrapped up in our own concerns that we forget the big picture: that God is passionately committed to forming a *distinct, new people* who will reflect his image in the world. We see this divine desire throughout the Bible.

One of the great promises repeated throughout Scripture is when God says:

> *"I will make you my own people, and I will be your God."*
>
> EXODUS 6:7

The God of the Bible is a God of relationship. He longs to be in relationship with us; he wants to be our God (see Revelation 21:3). But he doesn't just want to know us as individuals. He also wants to form a people on earth who recognisably belong to him.

That's why, in the Old Testament, there was so much focus on the people of Israel and also so much teaching on how they should conduct their national life. In those days, these were God's people and they needed to show the world what the living God was like – not least, through the way they cared for each other in their society. God had specially called Israel to be in a covenant* with him, that is, a binding relationship with promises. He wanted this 'covenant people' to look different from the other nations. Yet, because of disobedience, things in Israel often went from bad to worse; so the prophets began to predict a time when God would form a remnant of faithful Israelites, who alone would be God's true people (e.g. Isaiah 10:22–23).

Then Jesus came. Jesus was himself the perfect, faithful Israelite. In a strange sense, *he himself was* the 'people of God', the true Israel; as the Messiah he embodied in himself the hopes and destiny of the nation. And he began to draw around him a new 'remnant'. He chose twelve special followers (like the twelve tribes of ancient Israel), telling them that they were now the true 'flock' belonging to God (Luke 12:32). He welcomed unlikely people to follow him and shared table fellowship with others. Jesus was recruiting people to his cause. But he was *also re-founding the people of God around himself.* From now on, God's people would be defined not by background, but by faith in him, Jesus the Messiah.

As a result, the New Testament insists that not only Jews, but also Gentiles must, through Jesus, be allowed into God's people. Jesus had redefined God's people around himself. God's true people, now centred on Jesus, was to be made up of anyone who had faith in him. Jesus was the vine; his followers were the branches (John 15:5). Or, to use some of the apostles' other favourite pictures:

> *Jesus had redefined God's people around himself.*

- Jesus is the head; we are all his *body* (e.g. Ephesians 1:23; Colossians 1:19; 1 Corinthians 12:12–27).
- Jesus is the bridegroom; we are his *bride* (Ephesians 5:25–33; Revelation 21:2).
- Jesus is the chief foundation stone; we are the *building* constructed upon him (Ephesians 2:20; 1 Corinthians 3:11).
- Jesus is the builder; we are his *house* (Hebrews 3:3–6).
- Jesus is the eldest brother in a family; we are now brothers and sisters in his *family* (Romans 8:29; Hebrews 2:11–12).

In other words, there is an organic and unbreakable link between Jesus and his new people – as a head to its body, as a vine to its branches, as a brother to his siblings.

This explains why the New Testament writers were so passionate about the 'church' – that is, Jesus' new people. They knew that Jesus was passionately committed to his people – indeed organically linked to them! As Paul says:

> *Christ loved the church and gave his life for it ... for we are members of his body.*
>
> EPHESIANS 5:25, 30

> *He did this to dedicate the church to God ... in order to present the church to himself in all its beauty – pure and faultless. ... People never hate their own bodies. Instead, they feed them and take care of them, just as Christ does the church.*
>
> EPHESIANS 5:26–29

Jesus sees the church as his own body, as his bride. He wants her to be beautiful and to reflect his love. He wants those who see the church to see in her something of him – his true grace and love. So, even if we do not always love the church, Jesus clearly does! He loves her, indeed he died for her.

The apostles knew too from the Old Testament that their God was a community-creating God. They saw Jesus' mission as precisely intended to found and form such a new people for his Father – what we might call 'God's new society'. On the cross, Paul writes, Jesus 'gave himself for us, to rescue us from all wickedness and to make us a *pure people who belong to him* alone and are eager to do good' (Titus 2:14).

> He wants those who see the church to see in her something of him.

All this, then, should dispel any negative views we may have of the church or of being committed to Jesus' people. Once we grasp God's passionate determination to build a people of God, and once we see how Jesus is the organic centre of his church, we should find ourselves with a new resolve to demonstrate our own commitment to Jesus' followers. We should be people who care for each other's needs, do good, and do all we can to build up his church – never tearing it down.

There may still be some occasions when we may want to join others in saying, "Jesus *yes*, church *no!*" Yet, if God has called us to himself through Jesus, he is now calling us also to *love Jesus' church* and to play our part in making her what he wants her to be. She is, despite her failings, God's new people.

Loving God's people

Acts 2, then, describes several things all at once:

- the launch of the church;
- the establishment of God's new people;
- the founding of Jesus' family;
- the unveiling of his beautiful bride.

The fact that visitors from so many nations heard the Good News in their own tongue is a dramatic signal (given uniquely to mark this one-off event) to demonstrate that this new community will be a *truly international one* – an inclusive people, crossing boundaries, extending to the world's end, and overturning the mix-up of languages that, in biblical imagery, has cursed the world ever since the 'tower of Babylon' (see Genesis 11:1–9).

Acts 2 also shows us our response – that is, what the Holy Spirit wants to bring about in our own lives as a result. Jesus' followers committed themselves to each other in radical ways. They realised how much they had in common because of Jesus and his Spirit, and they then sought to express this fellowship in down-to-earth practice. They realised, in a word, that *loving Jesus means loving his people*.

This is not always easy. Indeed the subsequent story in Acts shows some of the difficulties the early Christians had: people backtracked on their commitments or started lying to each other; some began to feel overlooked or neglected by others; differences of strategy emerged; tensions grew between different nationalities and backgrounds (see Acts chapters 5–6; 15). Jesus' followers include many different types of people. Some we will naturally like and understand, others we will not! Also, many are hurting or sick, meaning that the church often feels like a hospital – made up of people who in different ways all need tender, loving care. Yet none of this can negate the vision (displayed before us so clearly in Acts 2) of what God wants to do – and indeed *can* do – when his Holy Spirit is truly at work among us.

Loving Jesus means loving his people.

All of this requires us to love. Where can we find sufficient resources for such great love? Not from us, of course, but thankfully from the Holy Spirit.

> *God has poured out his love into our hearts by means of the Holy Spirit, who is God's gift to us.*
>
> ROMANS 5:5

The Holy Spirit, already given to us, now becomes the channel for the outpouring of God's love. This is indeed a gift from God. As Paul explains when talking about the 'gifts' of the Holy Spirit, this Christ-like love (known as *agape** love) is the 'greatest' gift that God can place within us (1 Corinthians 13:13). So when he describes this love (see Box 7), we are to read his words – even though they are challenging – as describing *that which God's Spirit can produce in us*. Not for nothing is love the very first 'fruit of the Spirit' mentioned by Paul, when he describes these being produced in the lives of believers (Galatians 5:22). The same is true as we read some other New Testament passages in which we are commanded to love (see Box 7).

Box 7 — Some New Testament passages on God's call to love and unity

"And now I give you a new commandment: love each other. ... As I have loved you, so you must love one another."

JESUS WORDS IN JOHN 13:34

Love is patient and kind; it is not jealous or conceited or proud; love is not ill-mannered or selfish or irritable; love does not keep a record of wrongs; love is not happy with evil, but is happy with the truth. Love never gives up; and its faith, hope and patience never fail.

1 CORINTHIANS 13:4–7

You are the people of God; he loved you and chose you for his own. So then you must clothe yourselves with compassion, kindness, humility, gentleness and patience. Be tolerant with one another and forgive one another whenever any of you have a complaint against someone else. You must forgive one another just as the Lord has forgiven you. And to all these qualities add love, which binds all things together in perfect unity.

COLOSSIANS 3:12–14

This is how we know what love is: Christ gave his life for us. We too, then ought to give our lives for our brothers and sisters! Rich people who see a brother or sister in need, yet close their hearts against them, cannot claim that they love God. My children, our love should not just be words and talk; it must be true love, which shows itself in action.

1 JOHN 3:16–18

Whoever does not love does not know God, for God is love. ... This is what love is: it is not that we have loved God, but that he loved us and sent his Son to be the means by which our sins are forgiven. ... No one has ever seen God, but if we love one another, God lives in union with us, and his love is made perfect in us. ... God is love, and whoever lives in love lives in union with God and God lives in union with him. ... We love because God first loved us.

1 JOHN 4:8, 10, 12, 19

Help to carry one another's burdens, and you will obey the law of Christ.

GALATIANS 6:2

"May they be completely one, in order that the world may know that you sent me and that you love them as you love me."

JESUS' WORDS IN JOHN 17:23

The apostles give these commands, because they know we are disobedient and will not love if not commanded; but they also know that Jesus by his Spirit can supply the resources we need. As Augustine* once said, "Command what you will, O Lord; then give what you command!" With God's help, we can begin to fulfil Jesus' new command to love each other.

Note too how John insists that such loving must be practical – not just in words but also in action. Love *actually*. The first Christians discovered God had given them a whole new kind of love. If we have recently become a believing Christian, one of the sure signs of this will be the new love which we sense towards other believers. Yet one of the best ways of growing as a Christian is not just to *feel* this love, but also to put that love into practice! Love, after all, is not to be hoarded to ourselves, but rather to be gladly given away!

So the seventh building-block, as we follow Jesus, is all about loving Jesus' followers. We are to *share with Jesus' people* in practical ways, demonstrating the love of Christ.

Building-block 7

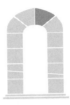

Share with Jesus' People – They are Now Your Family!

Worship His Majesty

They devoted themselves to ... prayer.

ACTS 2:42 NIV

The next theme we note from this key verse is that Jesus' followers instinctively began to worship God and to pray. They found that their new commitment to Jesus meant they now had a new relationship, not just with each other (expressed, as we have just seen, in fellowship) but also with God himself. Their lives could not help but be filled with prayer.

Inevitably, their focus was not just 'horizontal' but 'vertical'. Jesus had spoken about the need for us to love our neighbour as ourselves, but he had also made it clear what our first priority was to be: "Love the Lord your God with all your heart ..." (Mark 12:28–31, based on Deuteronomy 6:4–5 and Leviticus 19:18). Get *this* relationship right, he was implying, and then your other relationships will fall into place. So what we see in Acts 2 is the Holy Spirit helping those first believers with this 'vertical' dimension: he was helping them to worship.

Even more startling, the Spirit was helping them to worship *Jesus*. One of the most remarkable things in the early chapters of Acts is how the first believers, despite coming from a Jewish background, found themselves instinctively worshipping Jesus. After all, the very text which Jesus had quoted from Deuteronomy was the same one which underlined Jewish monotheism* – the belief in only one God: 'The LORD – and

> The Spirit was helping them to worship *Jesus*.

the LORD alone – is our God; ... *worship only him*' (Deuteronomy 6:4, 13). Yet here now were Jewish people worshipping Jesus! This was the clear implication of Peter's words here in Acts 2 which speak of Jesus as the 'Lord' exalted to the 'right-hand side of God' (verses 32–36). Such worship would be blasphemous in the eyes of many, but the first believers were led by the Holy Spirit to confess "Jesus is Lord" and to worship him.

We shall return below (in chapter 9) to what this reveals about Jesus' true identity – his somehow being identified with the glorious God who alone is to be worshipped. For now, however, we focus on what this means for Jesus' followers: we are called to a life of worship, and this includes worshipping Jesus himself who shares in God's glory. We are to worship King Jesus in all his royal power; we are to *worship his majesty*.

Worship, however, does not come easily to us. Jesus' encouragement that we should love God with all our heart implies that, as creatures made by God, we are created to worship him; so our emotions, our thinking, our energies are all designed to work best when they are touched and motivated by love for God. Yet, as sinful people, we so easily worship other people and other things.

Many in the West worship materialism, but Jesus clearly warned what this will do to our hearts:

> *Do not store up riches for yourselves here on earth, where moths and rust destroy. ... For your heart will always be where your riches are.*
>
> MATTHEW 6:19–21

Other things too can steal our hearts away from God: evil desires, greed, wrong relationships, selfish activities. Indeed, in the Bible, anything which comes between the believer and God is called an 'idol', a false object of our heart's hidden worship. But Jesus is now the one we must worship, and all other idols are to be thrown down in his name. 'My children,' writes the apostle John, 'keep yourselves safe from false gods [or idols]!' (1 John 5:21).

So the eighth building-block in the Christian life is to ensure that we give time to worship God, keeping Jesus enthroned as the ruler of our lives. When we come to Christ for the first time, this itself is an act of worship – as we 'turn away from idols to serve the true and living God' (1 Thessalonians 1:9). However, this turning to God must then continue on a daily basis, with worship becoming a recognisable hallmark of our lives. Worshipping God is to be a way of life – the very air that we breathe; it is to become

We were created for worship.

part of the very fabric of our personalities. After all, we were created for such worship.

Those first believers spent their time in prayer. They were also constantly 'praising God' (Acts 2:47), as this worship of God then flowed over into the whole of their lives, affecting all that they did. As Jesus' followers, our lives are to be characterised by worship.

Worship: the true and living God

This biblical perspective – that worship is about all our lives – may come as surprise. Many think that worship is somehow confined to Sundays or whenever we meet together with other Christians (i.e. what we do corporately). In fact, it includes what we do on our own and indeed what we do with every part of our lives.

The word 'worship' in English is associated with the word 'worthy'. Worship, then, is giving God his 'worth', acknowledging that, as our Creator, he is worthy of all our praise. Throughout the Bible, there are powerful pictures of God's awesome power and holiness, his majesty and sovereignty. He is portrayed as quite distinct from us his creatures – wholly 'other' and transcendent. He is the 'God of all grace', the One 'from whom and to whom are all things' (1 Peter 5:10; 1 Corinthians 8:6). In the Old Testament he is regularly described as 'God Almighty', the 'Holy One of Israel' who is 'enthroned on the praises of his people'.

In one of the most significant episodes in Scripture, Israel's God is revealed to the prophet Isaiah as 'high and exalted', surrounded by angelic beings who endlessly declare his praise:

> *Holy, Holy, Holy!*
> *The LORD Almighty is holy!*
> *His glory fills the world.*

ISAIAH 6:3

Isaiah's response to this vision encapsulates the kind of response which should come from all of us before such a holy God:

> *"There is no hope for me! I am doomed because every word that passes my lips is sinful."*

ISAIAH 6:5

It is a graphic picture of what worship should mean before this awesome God.

The good news, however, is that this is not the Bible's last word on the subject of worship. Because of God's grace, our worship of him can be transformed from a position of abject abasement to a position of close, even intimate, relationship.

Here, then, are three further points which we must grasp if ever we are to gain a biblical perspective on worship.

1. Worship of the holy God: present in our midst

> *Honour the* Lord *your God, worship only him. ... Do not worship other gods. ... If you do worship other gods, the* Lord's *anger will come against you like fire ... because the* Lord *your God, who is present with you, tolerates no rivals.*
>
> Deuteronomy 6:13–15

Here is a classic call within the Old Testament for God's people to worship him, but note the strange idea that this holy God is 'present' amongst his people. It reveals how God wants to be close to his people, indeed to be at the centre of their life.

Sinful human beings, of course, do not like this. As in the story of Adam and Eve (in Genesis 3), we disobey God's Word, trying to replace the worship of God with ourselves, putting ourselves on the 'throne' of our lives. We want ourselves to be 'like God' (Genesis 3:5), to usurp his role; we want to place ourselves, not God, at the centre.

Yet God will not let us do this. He will contend with us to regain his rightful place at the centre. This is seen, for example, in the book that follows Genesis in the Bible (Exodus) when, after delivering his people from Egypt and having given them his Ten Commandments, God then gave detailed instructions for the building of a worship space called the 'Tent of the Lord's Presence' (Exodus 24–31). Why was this so important? Because God wanted his people to be able to meet with him and to worship him. We might say, God's great acts of redemption and revelation are always designed to foster relationship. The God revealed at Mount Sinai is awesomely holy, but he longs to be worshipped and encountered.

Moreover, this Tent of the LORD's Presence was to be located at the *very centre* of Israel's camp. Israel's God wanted to be at the heart of his people's corporate life. This principle is seen again later, when the Temple in Jerusalem is established at the centre of Israel's national life (see e.g. Psalms 48; 122). From this, we learn that the living God wants to be at the very centre of his people, right there in the middle of their community. Thus, although God is all-glorious, he is not a God who is far away. On the contrary, he is the Holy One who yet longs to come awesomely close: God in our midst.

> *God's great acts of redemption and revelation are always designed to foster relationship.*

2. Worship of the holy God: approached through sacrifice

We have ... complete freedom to go into the Most Holy Place by means of the death of Jesus. He opened for us a new way, a living way, through the curtain. ... So let us come near to God with a sincere heart and a sure faith ...

HEBREWS 10:19–22

God's provision of the Temple in Jerusalem also gave his people a place where they could approach him. Despite his holiness and their sin, God established a sacrificial system through which he could forgive them. Relationship was restored through sacrifice. From this, we learn that we cannot just walk into God's presence, but must approach him *in the way he himself has determined* and with our sins forgiven.

For us, in the light of Jesus' coming and his sacrificial death on the cross (see above in chapter 2), this now means coming to God *only through Jesus' death*: we are to be 'purified from sin by the offering he made of his own body once and for all' (Hebrews 10:10). Indeed, because of the cross, we can gain an access into God's holy presence that was only hinted at within the Old Testament period. For when Jesus died, the Temple curtain (which had prevented worshippers from entering the Most Holy Place) was suddenly 'torn in two, from top to bottom' (Mark 15:38). The final barrier has been broken down. If previously there was a 'No Entry' sign, barring the way into God's full presence, then now, through the cross, it says in large letters, 'ALL WELCOME!'

New Testament worship is therefore marked by this great theme of our access into God's very presence: 'We have ... complete *freedom* to go in' (Hebrews 10:19). 'Now that we have been put right with God through faith, he has given us *access* by faith into this experience of God's grace' (Romans 5:1–2, my translation). 'It is through Christ that all of us ... are able to come in the one Spirit into the presence of the Father' (Ephesians 2:18).

3. Worship of the holy God: by his Spirit

Acts 2 also makes it abundantly clear that true worship can now only be brought about by the agency and presence of the Holy Spirit. Jesus had hinted at this great new reality earlier in his ministry:

> "The time is coming and is already here, when by the power of God's Spirit people will worship the Father as he really is, offering him the true worship that he wants. God is Spirit, and only by the power of his Spirit can people worship him as he really is."
>
> JOHN 4:23–24

We are to worship God (as other versions translate this) 'in spirit and in truth' (NIV). Jesus is teaching that, because of *his* coming (being himself 'the truth': John 14:6) and the coming of the *Spirit*, it will now be possible for anyone anywhere to worship God in a way that is acceptable and pleasing. As seen above in chapter 3, the Spirit also enables us to call God "*Abba*", that is, "Father! my Father!" and intercedes for us when 'we do not know how we ought to pray' (Romans 8:15, 26). It is the Holy Spirit who makes true worship possible.

Putting all this together, we can sense how God himself has provided the means whereby we can approach him in worship: he longs to come close, but we can only come close to him through Jesus' death and by the Spirit. We also sense the Trinitarian* nature of Christian worship; for this reason, the Greek Orthodox church defines worship neatly as being '*of* God the Father, *through* God the Son, *in* God the Holy Spirit'.

If Jesus is not Lord of all, then he is not Lord at all.

Worship in every aspect of our lives

By means of his Spirit, God is therefore calling people to the worship of Jesus. He want us to turn from ourselves, abandoning our idols, and to obey him truly. He wants us to be coming into his presence by the cross and (in reverse) to be welcoming his presence among us by his Spirit. God is to be at the centre of our lives.

Once we see this, we realise straightaway that such worship cannot be kept in some small, distinct corner of our lives. No, all our lives are to be given to this worship. If Jesus is not Lord *of all*, then he is not Lord *at all*. If becoming Jesus' follower is like opening the front door of our house to him (see chapter 1 above), we must remember that he must go on to be in charge of the whole house! There are, as it were, no 'rooms' (such as our family life or relationships, our hopes or fears) which he may not enter.

Consider these words of Paul:

> *So then, my brothers and sisters, because of God's great mercy to us I appeal to you: offer yourselves as a living sacrifice to God, dedicated to his service and pleasing to him. This is the true worship that you should offer. Do not conform yourselves to the standards of this world, but let God transform you inwardly by a complete change of your mind.*
>
> ROMANS 12:1–2

True worship, we see here, is a response: giving ourselves back to the God who has shown us his mercy. It is *total*: we are to give all of ourselves, including the physical and practical aspects of our lives (Paul speaks literally of offering 'our *bodies*'). And it is *continual*: we don't just do this in church, but we keep

Worship covers the whole of life.

offering ourselves to God, especially when challenged by temptations and the standards of this world. Worship covers the whole of life.

These verses also contain a great promise, which moves us on to see one of the great benefits of such worship. Of course, the primary reason for worshipping God is simply that our God is worthy of our worship. Yet God also knows that our worshipping *him* will benefit *us*. True worship, writes Paul, will be the means by which God can transform us and indeed completely change our minds. Many people have been damaged in their thinking or wounded in their spirits, but true worship can lead to healing and to a renewed mind. How does worship do this?

- It allows God's Spirit within us to be more effective.
- It helps keep Jesus truly at the centre, thus enabling us to do what Jesus would do and to think his thoughts.
- It removes our sinful selves from the throne of our lives and builds up our resistance towards the Evil One (see chapter 11).
- It gives us precious times of knowing how much we are loved by God, which then sets us free to be motivated not by self but by God's love.

God wants Christians to be more like Christ; he wants us to 'become like his Son' (Romans 8:29). How does he do this? By calling us to worship him.

So worship is to be theme of all our lives. That's why Paul can encourage us to 'pray at all times' (1 Thessalonians 5:17) – not because we are reciting prayers all day, but because *all our lives are soaked in prayer*. All our lives are to be lived in the Lord's presence. He says,

> *Everything you do or say should be done in the name of the*
> *Lord Jesus, as you give thanks through him to the Father.*
>
> COLOSSIANS 3:17

For Paul, the goal is a life of *total* worship.

Worship on our own: personal prayer

> *"When you pray, go to your room, close the door, and pray to*
> *your Father, who is unseen. And your Father, who sees what*
> *you do in private, will reward you."*
>
> MATTHEW 6:6

Once we have this vision of *all* our lives being 'worship', we can then see the importance of spending *some time each day* on our own consciously praying to God. For how can we live every moment of our day *as* worship (when we are also busy with other things), if we never spend some time *in* worship (when we are *not* busy with other things)? We are to take into our day the presence of the Lord whom we have already met, and with whom we have been in recent, focused communication.

So Jesus' followers need to find some time each day to talk with him. Many find early mornings are best; others prefer other times of the day, when they know they can be undisturbed and will be fresh enough to focus on God. But, whenever and wherever we pray, we can be sure that such times are very precious in God's sight. He is already there, delighted that we are seeking his face (see Psalm 27:8 NIV). We are to give time to this secret, unseen task — something that others will never know much about and for which we will seldom receive human praise. Yet, according to Jesus, this private worship is a vital part of following him; we will be rewarded by God giving us a deeper knowledge of his love and will.

When we talk with God, we can use our own words. Jesus here expressly encourages us not to "use a lot of meaningless words, as the pagans do" but to pray in a simple and heartfelt way (Matthew 6:7). At the same time, Jesus goes on to give us a model prayer (the 'Lord's Prayer'), which we would do well to learn, to use frequently, and indeed to develop as the framework for our own further prayers.

Box 8 – Prayer and worship

THE LORD'S PRAYER

> *Our Father in heaven, hallowed be your name.*
> *Your kingdom come, your will be done,*
>> *on earth as it is in heaven.*
> *Give us this day our daily bread.*
> *And forgive us our sins,*
>> *as we forgive those who sin against us.*
> *Lead us not into temptation,*
>> *but deliver us from evil.*
> *For yours is the kingdom, the power and the glory,*
>> *for ever and ever!*
> *Amen**

MATTHEW 6:9–13 (IN THE MODERN TRANSLATION USED IN MANY CHURCHES IN THE UK)

*THE **P.R.A.Y.** PRINCIPLE – FOUR KEY INGREDIENTS*
(both for personal prayer and public worship)

- **P**raise: worship God for who he is and seek to 'be thankful in all circumstances' (1 Thessalonians 5:18). See e.g. Psalms 98; 100; 103; 117; 148; 150.

- **R**epent: confess* your sins (1 John 1:9) and come to Jesus for forgiveness through his cross. See e.g. Psalms 32; 51; 95.

- **A**sk for others: intercede for other people and difficult situations in which you long for God's kingdom to 'come on earth as it is in heaven' (Matthew 6:10). See e.g. Psalms 20; 107; 121; see also Paul's prayers in Ephesians 1:15–23; Philippians 1:9–11; Colossians 1:9–14.

- ... and for **Y**ourself: at the end, ask for yourself for your 'daily bread', seek the fruit and gifts of the Spirit in your life, and bring to God any personal concerns of your own. 'Leave all your worries with him, because he cares for you' (1 Peter 5:7). See e.g. Psalms 22; 28; 38; 56; 63.

PAUL ON PRAYER

Don't worry about anything, but in all your prayers ask God for what you need, always asking him with a thankful heart. And God's peace, which is far beyond human understanding, will keep your hearts and minds safe in union with Christ Jesus.

PHILIPPIANS 4:6–7

Note how Jesus encourages us to begin and end our praying with a focus on God himself – his holiness, his kingdom and his glory. Note too how we can ask God for things, but these must include forgiveness for sin, and deliverance from evil. Finally, note that we can approach God truly as our Father, but that this is true, not just for me as an individual, but for any who call on God's name through Jesus: he is 'our Father'. This means there is a sense in which we never quite pray this prayer on our own, but are always part of Jesus' wider family.

Jesus has not given us only the Lord's Prayer. There is the whole of the Bible. This too (especially the Psalms, which formed Jesus' own prayer book) can give us words to speak to God when we have no words of our own.

And, of course, the Bible is also the place where we hear God speaking *to us*. Reading (or even reciting) a few words of Scripture can have a powerful effect, especially when we ask God's Spirit to be our teacher. It's so powerful to sense God speaking to us personally from his word! The Bible is like a letter from a friend, which we should open with enthusiasm. 'Every morning he makes me *eager* to hear what he is going to teach me' (Isaiah 50:4–5). So, as we open the Scriptures, we will begin to hear God's voice, and this in turn will fuel our prayers.

Some people find the **P.R.A.Y.** principle (see Box 8) to be a useful structure for their times of personal prayer. Others find keeping a personal journal helps them to look back over previous weeks and to note the answers to their prayers. Some find particular favourite locations are conducive to prayer; others take themselves off on 'prayer walks' where they talk with God as they walk. There is no one right way to pray! The important thing is to be both disciplined and reasonably creative, trying out different habits and finding out gradually what works best for you.

Whatever its precise form, then, this personal encounter with the Lord, this private worship of Jesus, is to be the secret powerhouse of our whole lives. For we can hardly be his followers, if we never talk to him, tell him we love him, or listen to him for his instructions.

Worship with others: corporate prayer

Christ's message [literally, 'the word of Christ'] in all its richness must live in your hearts. Teach and instruct each other with all wisdom. Sing psalms, hymns and sacred songs; sing to God with thanksgiving in your hearts.

COLOSSIANS 3:16

Finally, there is that worship which we offer to God when in the company of others — in small groups or in church services. In Acts 2, we see the believers continuing to *meet together* 'day after day', 'praising God' both in the Temple courts and in their homes (verses 46–47). We can worship God on our own, but 'corporate' or communal worship (when Jesus' followers expressly gather in his name) is also vitally important. There are several reasons for this.

First, Scripture tells us that we are not to be 'solo' Christians. We are not to 'give up the habit of meeting together' but rather to 'encourage one another' (Hebrews 10:25). Just as burning coals keep warm so long as they stay together, so too we need one another to keep 'warm' in the faith. A piece of coal, even if very hot originally, soon goes cold if left on its own.

More importantly, Jesus gave us this express promise:

> "Where two or three come together in my name, I am there with them."
>
> MATTHEW 18:20

This promise of divine presence ties in with what we learned about the presence of the Holy Spirit (in chapter 3 above) and about the 'fellowship of the Holy Spirit' (2 Corinthians 13:13; see chapter 7 above). In other words, Jesus by his Spirit is especially present when his followers meet together – this is when this fellowship becomes a spiritual reality. We need to meet together so that the Holy Spirit can work between us, and so that *Jesus can be seen in the ways we relate to one another*. If we do so, then visitors may be able to say (what Paul hoped would be said in Corinth): "Truly God is here among you!" (1 Corinthians 14:25).

So what should Jesus' followers do when they meet together? What are the vital ingredients for an authentic act of corporate Christian worship?

Perhaps the primary thing to be included is the public reading of Scripture and appropriate teaching from the Bible. Thus Paul (in the words from Colossians quoted above) talks about singing and thanksgiving only *after* he has first mentioned the importance of teaching and instruction. Hence, in Acts 2, the first thing to which the new believers devote themselves is 'the apostles' teaching' (see further in chapters 9 to 12 below). Christian worship is always a response to God's self-revelation. It is never to be the worship of ourselves or of our own bright ideas, but rather a turning towards God – to what he has said and done. It is always to be a means through which the 'word of Christ' may come to

Christian worship is always a response to God's self-revelation.

dwell in our hearts more powerfully. And for this, we will always need the Bible.

Once this is firmly in place, however, the **P.R.A.Y.** principle (Box 8) may once again be a useful guide. When next in a church service, it might be worth noting if and how these four things are taking place! In addition to the Bible readings and any talk or sermon:

- Are there hymns and prayers which **praise** God for his words and his deeds? Are there other opportunities too for giving thanks? If it is a communion service, there should be a central prayer (the Great Thanksgiving or Eucharist*), in which we thank God for Jesus' death; but on other occasions, someone may share a personal testimony to God's goodness.
- Is there a time for confession*, as together people come humbly before the Lord to **repent**?
- Are there opportunities to **ask** God for things, praying both for others and then for **yourself**? These may occur in 'set' prayers*, or perhaps when praying for one another after the service.

There may be other ingredients too. In Colossians, for example, Paul evidently expected a variety of different types of songs (psalms, hymns, sacred songs). Some of these may be more formal, others informal; some sung, as it were, *to one another* to encourage us to praise God, others expressly addressed *to God* (perhaps speaking in quite intimate and personal ways as we seek to enjoy his presence); some drawn from contemporary experience, others more obviously rooted in the Bible. There can be a wide variety here, even before we mention all the variety of accompanying music styles – some of which we may personally love, others of which we may not!

Meanwhile, as we read in 1 Corinthians, Paul clearly expected a wide variety of 'spiritual gifts' to be in evidence. For example,

> *A message full of wisdom, ... a message full of knowledge, ... faith, ... the power to heal, ... the power to work miracles, ... the gift of speaking God's message; ... the ability to tell the difference between gifts that come from the Spirit and those that do not; ... the ability to speak in strange tongues, and ... the ability to explain what is said.*
>
> 1 Corinthians 12:8–10

Yes, he was concerned about the way these gifts could be abused in ungodly ways, and so spoke about the 'greatest gift' – that of love (1 Corinthians 13; see above chapter 7). Yet Paul clearly envisaged that Christian worship-gatherings would sometimes include the use of some of these gifts:

> When you meet for worship, one person has a hymn, another a teaching, another a revelation from God, another a message in strange tongues, and still another the explanation of what is said.
>
> 1 CORINTHIANS 14:26

So there may be such signs of God's Holy Spirit at work. This should not surprise us, for the Holy Spirit lives within each believer and wants to help the body of Christ to be a living, dynamic force. Our part may then be simply to come to public worship with an attitude of expectancy and to be ready to share what we think God has been doing in our lives. We are not to be passengers, but must come ready to contribute.

Come to public worship with an attitude of expectancy.

We must also come in a spirit of humility, willing to be taught and led by those in authority, and never in a disruptive spirit:

> None of you should be looking to your own interests, but to the interests of others. ... Everything must be of help to the church ... because God does not want us to be in disorder but in harmony and peace. ... Everything must be done in a proper and orderly way.
>
> 1 CORINTHIANS 10:24; 14:26, 33, 40

As we welcome God's Spirit amongst us, our goal will always be to do that which is helpful for others and which builds up our brothers and sisters in their faith (1 Corinthians 14:17).

The apostles of Jesus want his people to make sure they regularly worship God together. Sometimes we may not feel like it, but that is precisely the point. Worship is not about *us* and our *feelings*; it is all about *God* and his *worth*. So sometimes worship will indeed be a matter of the will, not just of the heart. Yet, amazingly, so often when we truly give ourselves to worship, our hearts are strangely warmed – we come out feeling quite different. This is a happy by-product of worship, but it is not its primary goal. 'Praise the LORD,' we are commanded, 'and do not forget how kind he is' (Psalm 103:2).

So the eighth building-block in the Christian life is to give a priority to worshipping the Lord Jesus: we are to *worship his majesty*. The first believers devoted themselves to 'prayer', and so should we. Worship is to be our lifeblood. It is what we were made for. And it is what one day, according to Revelation, we will be doing for all eternity:

Day and night they never stop singing:

'Holy, holy, holy,
   is the Lord God Almighty,
who was, who is, and who is to come.' ...

And I heard every creature in heaven, on earth, in the world below, and in the sea – all living beings in the universe – and they were singing:

'To him who sits on the throne
   and to the Lamb,
be praise and honour, glory and might,
   for ever and ever!'

REVELATION 4:8; 5:13

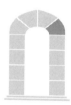

Building-block 8

Worship His Majesty
– It's What You were Made For!

Follow His Teaching

They devoted themselves to ... the apostles' teaching.

Acts 2:42 NIV

We see in Acts 2 that, for the new believers, it was a top priority to discover the 'apostles' teaching'. They had committed themselves to following Jesus as king but, right now, they only knew a tiny part of his royal truth. We too may have decided to follow Christ – perhaps for a wide variety of different reasons – but there remains so much more to discover about him. So each of our final chapters will unpack more of the apostles' teaching – about who Christ is (Christian *belief*); about how we should live for him (Christian *behaviour*); and, finally, about what are his future purposes for us (Christian *hope*).

The example of those first believers is one of humility. They were ready to be taught. In the West today, teachers are often ridiculed and disobeyed – people think *they* know best and so are difficult to teach. In other cultures, however, teachers are often greatly respected; people value learning and are glad to sit at others' feet, being honest about what they do not know. This humble attitude is the one Jesus is looking for in his followers:

"If you love me, you will obey my teaching."

John 14:15

Those baptised in Jesus' name are 'to obey everything [he] commanded' (Matthew 28:20). So those first believers committed themselves in advance to obey anything that the apostles passed on to them from the lips of Jesus. But will we do the same? Will we humbly submit our minds and wills to him – truly sitting at his feet?

Here we hit a strange thing. Luke does not say that those first believers devoted themselves to the teaching of *Jesus*. No, they devoted themselves to the teaching of *the apostles*. Partly, this is for the obvious reason that Jesus himself was no longer there in Jerusalem. Yet it is also Luke's way of making a vitally important point: precisely because Jesus is no longer here, the way we submit to *his* teaching, is to submit ourselves to the teaching of *his apostles*. We saw above (in chapter 4) how Jesus commissioned the apostles as his special messengers, authorising them to teach his truth. So humility before Jesus requires humility before his messengers. For us today (when those messengers have long since died), this means in practice a humility towards that which they have writen – that is, the New Testament.

> Because Jesus is no longer here, the way we submit to *his* teaching, is to submit ourselves to the teaching of *his apostles*.

If we are to be devoted to the apostles' teaching, then, because of our love for Jesus, we will love the New Testament (and the Bible as a whole), submitting our minds to its truth and committing ourselves to obeying its commands.

So the ninth building-block as we walk in the Jesus Way is to *follow his teaching* – not just what Jesus taught during his earthly ministry, but also that which he teaches us through the apostles and the rest of Scripture.

The Creed: a summary of the apostles' teaching

But what exactly did the apostles teach? The New Testament was drawn together over about 50 years (c. AD 30–80) from the works of different authors writing in different contexts and in different styles. It is a colourful book, far from monochrome. This means it is not entirely straightforward to summarise. God has chosen to reveal his will in a document which is far more interesting than, say, a legal code. It is a document brimming with light and life; it is also fundamentally a story, with a fascinating plot line which draws us into its world, and which demands a response.

Yet this living quality of the New Testament must not be taken as meaning that it contains no definite teaching on any subject. No, it gives a coherent answer on all the subjects that God wants us to know about. Ask the New Testament a reasonable question and it will give you an authoritative answer! What it does mean, however, is that, ever since its composition, believers have rightly been trying to summarise the apostles' teaching in brief, systematic ways.

In the early days, these summaries were called 'rules of faith', but in due course, they came to be called creeds* (*credo* means 'I believe' in Latin). Their intention was never to add to the New Testament but rather to summarise it, expounding its essential inner teaching. They were intended as reliable guides *within which* to enjoy the New Testament's teaching – effectively warning that those who came up with quite different ideas had misread it.

The same is true today. The Bible is an open book for everyone, but individuals can misinterpret its teaching. The creeds then give us a tried and tested way in which the wider body of Christian believers can 'hold firmly to the true words' of the apostles' teaching (see 2 Timothy 1:13). They are safeguards – like fences around playing fields, or like railway lines. Or they are like wise parents, pointing out where true freedom lies: "This truly is what it means – trust us!" In other words, if we are reading the Bible appropriately (with faith in Christ at the centre), then the teaching contained in the creeds is what we will find.

In this chapter, then, we will focus on the text of the so-called Nicene Creed* (see Box 9a). As a creed, its focus is deliberately on what we are to *believe* (not on Christian practice). Yet it remains a brilliant summary of the apostles' teaching in this particular area, summarised under three main headings.

Box 9a – The Nicene Creed

1. *We believe in One God, the Father, the Almighty,*
   maker of heaven and earth,
   of all that is, seen and unseen.

2. *We believe in one Lord, Jesus Christ,*
   the only Son of God,
   eternally begotten of the Father,
   God from God, Light from Light,
   true God from true God,
   begotten, not made, of one Being with the Father;
   through whom all things were made.

For us and for our salvation he came down from heaven,
   was incarnate from the Holy Spirit and the Virgin Mary
   and was made man.

For our sake he was crucified also for us under Pontius Pilate;
he suffered death and was buried.
On the third day he rose again in accordance with the Scriptures;
he ascended into heaven
and is seated at the right hand of the Father.
He will come again in glory to judge the living and the dead,
and his kingdom will have no end.

3. We believe in the Holy Spirit,
the Lord, the giver of life,
who proceeds from the Father,
who with the Father and the Son is worshipped and glorified,
who has spoken through the prophets.

We believe in one, holy, catholic and apostolic church.
We acknowledge one baptism for the forgiveness of sins.
We look for the resurrection of the dead
and the life of the world to come.

Amen

Believe: in God the Father

The apostles were convinced that they were bringing Good News from the one true God. In their ancient world, where people believed in many 'gods', they affirmed that in Jesus Christ we truly see the action of the true and living God. Hence the first section of the Nicene Creed which categorically proclaims Christian *mono*theism – that there is only one God.

This God is described as the 'maker of heaven and earth, of all that is, seen and unseen'. This matches the apostles' teaching that God is our 'Creator' (1 Peter 4:19, based on passages such as Genesis 1 – 2 and Isaiah 40). This is important. It means that we should value God's created world – this planet earth and our environment. It also means that, if God in Jesus is offering us salvation, his purpose will never be somehow to remove us from the created world (as if the created world was 'bad' and inherently evil); no, God plans to bring about a renewed creation (see below in chapter 12). The God of *redemption* is also the God of *creation*, and we should never drive a wedge between the two. God is restoring creation, not abandoning it.

It also means that God is not seeking to destroy that which is human. No, he created us as human beings. Despite what many people think, to become a follower of Jesus never means we become *less* human. On the contrary, we at last are becoming truly human, as God always intended us to be; we are following Jesus who is the true Human, the most authentic human being that has ever lived (that's why he's described by Paul as the new 'Adam' in Romans 5 and 1 Corinthians 15).

These were all key points which the early Christians had to defend when faced with some false teachers (known as the Gnostics*) who saw created matter as evil, and who saw 'salvation' as essentially a means of escape from the material world. These Gnostic thinkers often drove another wedge too – this time between the 'god' of the Old Testament and the 'god' of the New. They caricatured the Old Testament 'god' as a lesser god, or a god of evil intent, or a god overly concerned with physical matter.

The apostles would have been horrified at this caricature. The heart of their teaching was that the God seen in Jesus was to be identified 100 per cent with the God known to Israel. Jesus had brought the Old Testament story to its climax, and Jesus' God was truly the 'God of Abraham, Isaac, and Jacob' (see e.g. Matthew 22:32; Acts 3:13). Hence the Creed's use of Old Testament terminology at this point: 'One God' (Deuteronomy 6:4); 'the Almighty' (Psalm 91:1); 'maker of heaven and earth' (Psalm 121:2). *Jesus does not introduce us to a new 'god'* (the Creed is effectively saying), but rather *reveals, in a new and powerful way, the God known in the past within Israel.*

In fact, this clear identity between the God of Israel and the God of Jesus undergirds everything the apostles teach about God. They deliberately underscore what was revealed in the Old Testament, namely that God is an invisible, eternal, glorious Being, sovereign over his world, utterly faithful in his purposes, holy, righteous, wise and good. Just as in Old Testament times, so in the New Testament era, God is full of 'compassion and pity' and 'constant love'.

> *"I am the Lord, and I show compassion and pity."*
>
> Exodus 33:19

> *The Lord is merciful and loving,*
>   *slow to become angry and full of constant love.*
>
> Psalm 103:8

Even so, he is still the 'righteous Judge' (1 Peter 2:23). Thus, in both Testaments, God is simultaneously the God of judgement and the God of love. If the New Testament speaks more freely concerning God's love, this is only because God's coming in Jesus has revealed this love so dramatically and in a new, unexpected way. Jesus' coming does not negate God's previous judgement, nor does it deny his previous love.

What Jesus' coming *does* introduce – in a way that is not really seen in the Old Testament but is still consistent with it – is the notion of God as Father. This distinctive apostolic teaching is included in the Creed in two senses. First, God is the 'Father of our Lord Jesus Christ' (1 Peter 1:3); there is, in the eternal heart of God, a fatherly relationship towards his unique Son. Yet, secondly, this father's heart now reaches out to include us: as we are adopted by faith into God's family, we too become his sons and daughters, and we can dare to call God "*our* Father" (see above in chapters 2, 3 and 8). This powerful privilege, brought about through the Good News, is proclaimed at the start of the Creed, because it is the bedrock (and indeed the goal) of the apostles' teaching.

> *In both Testaments, God is simultaneously the God of judgement and the God of love.*

Believe: in God the Son

At the centre of the apostles' teaching was Jesus himself – the fact that this human being was yet divine, and also that he had entered into the real world of human history for our rescue. This explains why the central, major part of the Creed focuses on the person and work of Jesus – that is, who he truly is and what he truly did.

Concerning the *work* of Jesus, the Creed is comparatively brief, mentioning his birth, suffering, death, resurrection and ascension but with little comment. In its phrases there is clearly a concern to ward off any Gnostic denials about the sombre reality of Jesus' suffering and death: he 'was buried' (truly dead, placed in a physical tomb) and this all took place 'under Pontius Pilate*' (the Roman governor's name serving to anchor these events in the real, physical world). It also states categorically (though with little explanation) that these events were 'for our salvation', 'for our sake' and 'in accordance with the Scriptures' (for my own explanation, see chapters 1 and 2).

Its greater emphasis, however, is upon the *person* of Jesus (a topic now known as Christology*) – not least because this was the key point under dispute at the time of the Creed's composition.

The apostles had said many amazing, bold things about Jesus, which the Creed here has to summarise in a few words. Whilst never denying that Jesus was truly human, the apostles had asserted that Jesus must be identified in some way with *God himself*. They had made this key point in different ways (see Box 9b):

Box 9b – The apostles' teaching on Jesus' identity

- He had been born in a unique way, from a virgin mother, by the power of the Holy Spirit (Matthew 1:20; Luke 1:35).

- He had claimed God's authority to forgive sins and to be the equivalent of a new Temple (Mark 2:5–11; John 2:19–21).

- He 'did not sin' (Hebrews 4:15), and so truly and perfectly revealed God's light (John 8:12).

- He had performed numerous 'works of power' or 'miracles' throughout his ministry (e.g. Acts 10:38) and had himself been raised from the dead (see above, chapter 1).

- He had truly been 'sent by God' – but clearly in a way that was different from God's previous 'sending' of the prophets (Hebrews 1:1–3; Galatians 4:4; 1 John 4:10).

- He was, in a unique sense, the true Son of God and shared in God's title as the Lord (see above, chapter 1); his status could thus be contrasted with that of mere humans (Galatians 1:1–2).

- He had been exalted to the Father's 'right-hand side' (Acts 2:33; Hebrews 1:3), where he was now 'seated on God's throne' and was the rightful object of human worship (Matthew 2:11; 14:33; 28:17; Philippians 3:3; Revelation 5:13; Revelation 19:6–10).

- He did things that, according to Old Testament, belonged to God alone – not least sharing in God's acts of creation and judgement (John 1:3; Colossians 1:16; John 5:27; also Philippians 2:11).

- He was an eternal being who, as a king, was establishing an eternal kingdom (Luke 1:32; 1 Corinthians 15:24); so, on occasion, he could appropriately be called 'God' (Romans 9:5 NIV; John 1:1; 20:28).

- He had been eternally present with God as 'the Father's only Son' (John 1:14), he was an 'exact likeness of God's own being' (Hebrews 1:3) and 'equal with God' (Philippians 2:6).

- He then 'became a human being' — or (as in many translations) 'was incarnate' (see John 1:1–14). On this last point, the apostles were correcting the false teaching of some Docetic* groups who denied Jesus had truly been human.

The Creed picks up many of these ideas ('Lord', 'Son of God', 'light', 'judge', 'kingdom') but gives special emphasis to the aspects of the apostles' teaching mentioned in these last two points – declaring that Jesus was 'eternally begotten ... not made', and then 'was made man'. At the time of the Creed's compilation (and especially in its Greek, not Jewish, context), there was a real need to answer people's questions about Jesus' inherent being — who *he truly was* in his own person. These New Testament verses helpfully answered that question. Other verses had shown how Jesus was effectively *functioning* as God and sharing in God's actions and activity (still an extraordinary claim, when made by monotheistic Jews!); but these verses spoke about Jesus' *essential being*. It was not just that he *did* the things of God, but he truly *was* God! Hence the Creed's assertion that Jesus really was 'of one substance' (*homo-ousios**) with the Father — a word they coined to express this apostolic teaching that Jesus really did *share in God's eternal being* (or 'substance').

So the Creed is teaching precisely what the New Testament also had taught, namely:

- Jesus is unique: truly human but truly divine;
- this God-Man came down from heaven for our salvation ... and became a human being;
- he is now seated at the right-hand side of the Father.

This claim for Jesus stands out starkly in our modern world. It's an unpopular truth, making Jesus quite different from other religious leaders and revealing God to be no vague, absent figure but rather someone who has come worryingly close. We might be tempted to think that it would be easier to 'water down' this message. Perhaps — not least when we are accused of arrogance or bigotry — it might be best to focus on Jesus' brilliant teaching as an authentic human being, whilst gradually abandoning this bizarre teaching from his apostles about his divinity.

But the Creed puts up a fence here and says, 'Don't go there!' It reminds us what Christians down the ages have always believed, as they recited the Creed (Sunday by Sunday). And it warns us that any interpretation of the New Testament which overlooks this teaching about Jesus has effectively lost the plot. This is what the apostles taught, and any followers of Jesus today must submit themselves 'to the apostles' teaching' – *especially on this vital, central, issue as to who Jesus is!* For Jesus does not want us, as his followers, to be concocting our own imaginary ideas about him, but rather to be enjoying the true portrait of him given to us by his special messengers. That way we can truly *follow the true Jesus* – not our own wishful thinking.

Believe: in God the Holy Spirit – and the Trinity

The Creed's final section begins with a focus on the Holy Spirit. The apostles' full teaching concerning the Holy Spirit was summarised above in chapter 3. Here, however, we note that the Creed wants particularly to underline their teaching (seen e.g. in John 14–16) that the Spirit is a divine Person. Thus, although he might be viewed as having a lesser status (he 'proceeds from the Father'), the Holy Spirit is yet to be worshipped; indeed he is the effective source of all spiritual life and is to be identified with the Lord.

He has also 'spoken through the prophets'. This again affirms the *eternal nature* of the Spirit: he did not come into existence at Pentecost (see Acts 2), but was at work in the Old Testament period, especially in Israel's prophets. It also points us to the truth that God's communication with human beings is always by means of his Spirit (1 Corinthians 2:10–12). Moreover, it underlines that Scripture (both Old and New Testaments) is the place where we find the faithful deposit of the Spirit's communication – God's eternal words for all people, breathed out by the Spirit. For if the Old Testament prophets were truly inspired by the Spirit, how much more is this true of those writing in the days of the New Covenant*? As a result, we may fairly conclude: what the Holy Spirit says, God says; and what the Holy Spirit says is now found in Scripture (see above, chapter 4).

The Creed closes with some brief affirmations about the church (it is one, holy, catholic* and apostolic) and about baptism (for the forgiveness of sins). These remind us that:

- believers in Jesus must be baptised (see Appendix C);
- when this happens, they are entering into a community, which is to be marked by repentance for sins, by holiness of life, and by faithfulness to the apostles' teaching and mission;
- this community is a worldwide family ('cath-olic' means effectively 'all around the world'); believers thus belong to an amazing phenomenon, which is not local but global!

Finally, the Creed closes with an appropriate flourish, looking forward to 'the resurrection of the dead and the life of the world to come' – all revealed to us through the resurrection of Jesus (see further below in chapter 12). Christian belief thus works itself out in action and is a powerful message that affects all our lives: forgiveness from the *past*, hope for the *future*, and for the *present* a life lived in company with all those who have been called to be part of Jesus' new people.

As we look back over the whole Creed, however, what leaps out at us is its threefold structure: it summarises the apostles' teaching in a Trinitarian* form rooted in the nature of God revealed as Father, Son and Holy Spirit. This creedal commitment to the Trinity (God known in three Persons) is often challenged. "Perhaps," it is argued, "this so-called 'trinity' is an unbiblical addition to the Bible, never actually taught in the New Testament!" However, the Creed is accurately reflecting the New Testament, which itself speaks plainly in the direction of the Trinity (see Box 9c).

Box 9c – The apostles' teaching on the Trinity

FROM PAUL

The grace of the Lord Jesus Christ, the love of God, and the fellowship of the Holy Spirit be with you all.

2 CORINTHIANS 13:13

There are different kinds of spiritual gifts, but the same Spirit gives them. There are different ways of serving, but the same Lord is served. There are different abilities to perform service, but the same God gives ability to everyone.

1 CORINTHIANS 12:4–6

God has poured out his love into our hearts by means of the Holy Spirit. ... God has shown us how much he loves us – it was while we were still sinners that Christ died for us! ... If the Spirit of God, who raised Jesus from death, lives in you, then he who raised Christ from death will also give life.

ROMANS 5:5, 8; 8:11 (SEE ALSO EPHESIANS 2:18)

FROM PETER

Let us give thanks to the God and Father of our Lord Jesus Christ. ... This was the time to which Christ's Spirit was pointing, in predicting the sufferings of Christ.

1 PETER 1:3, 11

FROM JOHN

God ... lives in union with us, because he has given us his Spirit. And we have seen ... that the Father sent his Son to be the Saviour of the world.

1 JOHN 4:13–14

The verses in Box 9c are worth reading carefully. Although the apostles do not use the actual word 'Trinity', it is evident that, at an almost unconscious level, their thoughts about God are taking a threefold form. So, although their experience of God as three Persons may have preceded their need to defend this truth (or to describe it with academic formulations), they clearly believed in what we now know as the Trinity. In fact, the apostles would have seen the Trinity as a fundamental truth, underpinning all their teaching. For, if Jesus was not divine, and the Spirit did not truly lead to encounter with God himself, then their message was not Good News at all.

So Bible-believing Christians are those who know God as a Trinity. We remember Jesus' own words when he spoke about the Spirit (see Box 3a) and especially when he said we should baptise people "in the name of the Father, the Son, and the Holy Spirit" (Matthew 28:19). And we then recognise that the compilers of the Creed were actually being faithful to the apostles' teaching when they too spoke of God in a Trinitarian way. For this is truly who God *is*!

> *The apostles would have seen the Trinity as a fundamental truth, underpinning all their teaching.*

Conclusion

As Jesus' followers, then, we are to give ourselves to the apostles' teaching. In this chapter, we have seen how the Nicene Creed accurately summarises some of that teaching, especially what they taught us to *believe* about God. In the following three chapters, we will unpack some further (perhaps more obviously practical) aspects of the apostles' teaching. For now, however, we close by remembering some words of Jesus that highlight the vital link between his truth and true freedom.

Jesus, who himself *is* the truth (John 14:16), has ensured that his special messengers, the apostles, also give us *truths that are reliable* – teaching that comes with Jesus' approval, inspired by the Spirit. He wants us then to give ourselves to this teaching because it ultimately comes from him. Yet this is also because, as he said, "If you obey my teaching, you will know the truth, and the truth will set you free" (John 8:31–32). Jesus' truth (and the apostles' teaching about Jesus) is truly liberating. Others may suggest that true freedom comes from doing what we want, but Jesus sees this as a form of slavery: "everyone who sins is a slave of sin" (verse 34). If we want freedom, it is found instead in serving Jesus and submitting ourselves to his truth – his service, as they say, is perfect freedom! So...

- Will we, for Jesus' sake, submit ourselves to the apostles' teaching and commit ourselves in advance to believe and obey what they taught?
- Will we pray for those who teach the faith, that they too may be true to this teaching, and ourselves encourage others to follow this teaching?

This is vital. The ninth building-block, then, in growing as a follower of Jesus is to ensure we *follow his teaching*, and so experience the great liberty that it brings.

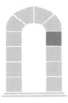

Building-block 9

Follow His Teaching
– It's the Only Way to Freedom!

Live His Life

Many miracles and wonders were being done by the apostles. ... All the believers ... shared their belongings, according to what each one needed. Day after day they met as a group ... praising God, and enjoying the good will of all the people.

ACTS 2:43–47

Jesus' first followers, as we have seen from Acts 2, devoted themselves to the apostles' teaching. This would clearly have included instructions, not just about Christian belief, but also about how to live in Jesus' new kingdom and under his rule. What we are seeing in Acts is evidently not just changed *minds* but radically altered *lives*. There is a new power, a new purpose, a new praising – altogether a new outpouring of love and life.

We could have guessed as much. In his own life, Jesus had shown a whole new way of being human – living in the power of the Spirit and establishing a pattern for life in God's kingdom. So to be a follower of this Jesus was always going to involve a change of lifestyle – indeed it means having our life turned upside down! And that's what we see in that first community of believers on the day of Pentecost: the birth of a whole new experiment in risky, Jesus-shaped, living.

> *The birth of a whole new experiment in risky, Jesus-shaped, living.*

Today, in just the same way, the Risen Jesus wants us to live *his* way and not ours. It is, after all, the Jesus Way. The opening message of his preaching was: "Turn away from your sins" (Mark 1:15). Jesus wants people to abandon their own agendas and follow his, to be changed from the inside out, to find both their minds and hearts transformed by his values. So Jesus wants to teach us what to do; as our king, he wants us, his subjects, to obey; as our leader, he wants his followers to ... follow. He doesn't just want us to *believe* the truth, but actually to *be* and *do* the truth!

We often squirm at this point. We like to focus on aspects of the Christian faith that suit us well (perhaps God's free forgiveness or his grace) and dismiss its practical challenges. We can even start labelling any who emphasise such obedience as 'legalists' or 'moralists'. Yet Jesus' apostles are quite clear: their frequent teaching about God's grace must never be taken as an excuse to sin or to be careless about our lifestyles; faith in Jesus is vital, but so too is obedience. It is "those who accept my commandments and obey them", Jesus says, who "are the ones who love me" (John 14:21).

So the tenth building-block in following Jesus is ... to follow Jesus! That is, to do what he says, to live our lives *as he would live them if he were us* – that is, to live *his* life. In every situation the vital question becomes "**W.W.J.D. – W**hat **W**ould **J**esus **D**o?" Or, as the apostle John puts it, 'those who say that they remain in union with God *should live just as Jesus Christ did*' (1 John 2:6). Are we willing to give ourselves to this key aspect of the apostles' teaching?

Walking the talk: obeying Jesus' commands

In fact, John's words might be even better translated as, 'We should walk as he walked.' The Bible often uses this picture of 'walking' to describe the believer's lifestyle. Clearly, what God wants is walkers, not just talkers. Do we, as they say, 'walk the talk'? 'Do not deceive yourselves,' writes James, 'by just listening to his word; instead, put it into practice' (James 1:22). Or, as Jesus himself had said:

> "Not everyone who calls me 'Lord, Lord' will enter the kingdom of heaven, but only those who do what my Father in heaven wants them to do. ...
> So then, anyone who hears these words of mine and obeys them is like a wise person who built his house on rock. ...
> But anyone who ... does not obey them is like a foolish person who built his house on sand."
>
> MATTHEW 7:21, 24, 26

This severe warning comes at the end of Jesus' Sermon on the Mount (Matthew 5 – 7). Box 10a gives us a list of the commands in that famous sermon, which he expects us to obey.

Box 10a – Challenges for life: a selection of Jesus' teaching from Matthew's gospel

FROM THE SERMON ON THE MOUNT (MATTHEW 5 – 7)

"Happy are those who are humble, ... merciful to others, ... pure in heart. ... Your light must shine before people, so that they will see the good things you do and praise your Father in heaven. ... Whoever is angry ... will be brought to trial."

5:5, 7, 8, 16, 22

"Anyone who looks at a woman and wants to possess her is guilty of committing adultery with her in his heart. ... If a man divorces his wife, for any cause other than her unfaithfulness, then he is guilty of making her commit adultery if she marries again. ... Do not take revenge on someone who wrongs you. ... Love your enemies and pray for those who persecute you. ... You must be perfect – just as your Father in heaven is perfect!"

5:28, 32, 39, 44, 48

"Make certain that you do not perform your religious duties [giving, praying, fasting] in public so that people will see what you do. ... Do not store up riches for yourself here on earth. ...You cannot serve both God and money. ... Do not start worrying ... Instead, be concerned above everything else with the kingdom of God."

6:1, 19, 24, 31, 33

"Do not judge others. ... Do for others what you want them to do for you."

7: 1,12

FROM LATER IN THE GOSPEL (CHAPTERS 15 – 28)

"From the heart come the evil ideas which lead someone to kill, commit adultery, and do other immoral things; to rob, lie, and slander others."

15:19

"See that you don't despise any of these little ones. ... Forgive your brother from your heart."

18:10, 35

"Whoever makes himself great will be humbled, and whoever humbles himself will be made great. ... On the outside you appear good to everybody, but inside you are full of hypocrisy and sins."

23:12, 28

"Whenever you did this for one of the least of these members of my family, you did it for me!"

25:40

"Teach them to obey everything I have commanded you."

28:20

Such a list may leave us all feeling pretty weak (indeed, this may be part of Matthew's point – Jesus' high standards drive us to our knees). However, in the very heart of Matthew's gospel, we find another, surprising command which contains a key secret:

> *"Come to me, all of you who are tired from carrying heavy loads, and I will give you rest. Take my yoke and put it on you, and learn from me, because I am gentle and humble in spirit; and you will find rest. For the yoke I will give you is easy, and the load I will put on you is light."*
>
> MATTHEW 11:28–30

Jesus says that, when we believe in him ('come to him') and bring our lives under his control ('take his yoke'), then we will have 'rest'. How can this be, when his commands seem so heavy?

Living the life: the amazing secret

The answer, so the apostles affirm, is that he gives us his rest through placing his own powerful life within us. Yes, Jesus commands us to live like him – to live our lives as though he were us. Yet we cannot do this in our own strength. That's where the Good News of both the resurrection and the Spirit come to the fore. Jesus is now alive and, by his Spirit, he is able to place his own new life within us. We can begin to 'live his life' because he himself is 'living his life' within us!

The apostle John is so helpful here. Despite his challenge that believers must walk as Jesus walked (see above), he concludes his letter with exactly this point: 'his commands are not too hard for us, because every child of God is able to defeat the world' (1 John 5:3–4). Why? Because anyone, who is a child of God, through faith in Jesus (5:5), now has God's Spirit dwelling in them: they live 'in union with God and God lives in union with them' (4:15). Believers have a unique resource and power within them: the life of God himself!

> *We can begin to 'live his life' because he himself is 'living his life' within us!*

The Christian life is truly meant to be Christ's life – Christ's life lived in and through us. We will therefore need Jesus' grace each and every day – not just for our forgiveness but indeed for any living at all! And this remains true, however many years we have been following Jesus. For, as Jesus warned us,

> *"Those who remain in me, and I in them, will bear much fruit; for you can do nothing without me."*
>
> JOHN 15:5

That's the key: with Jesus living within us by his Spirit, things become possible that previously were beyond our reach.

What we are seeing in Acts 2 (and indeed throughout the whole book of Acts) is the outworking of *Jesus' own life and power* – now released in and through his followers. The ancient world was being hit by a surge of divine life, flowing out through 'Jesus-indwelt' believers. Not for nothing, then, did we note in chapter 3 that today some people suggest a better name for The Acts of the Apostles is instead The Acts of *Jesus*. For it is the story of *his continued life and power* – now seen *within* his followers.

> *The Christian life is truly meant to be Christ's life – Christ's life lived in and through us.*

Let's observe, then, through studying Box 10b what happens once Jesus' Spirit is 'poured out' (Acts 2:17–18), enabling those first believers to begin to live out Jesus' risen life.

Box 10b – Living Jesus' life: selections from Acts

- Previously timid followers become brave and speak out in his name before crowds and interrogators (2:14; 4:8–21, 29–30; 5:21–32; 17:13–21; 18:12–17).

- When suffering persecution, they even find a deep joy within them, 'because God had considered them worthy to suffer disgrace for the sake of Jesus' (5:41; note Stephen's example in 6:8 – 7:60); they find themselves in prison but are able to sleep calmly and sing hymns before they are miraculously rescued (12:6–19; 16:23–40).

- Sometimes they are given power to heal, performing 'wonders and miracles' (3:6–7; 4:30; 13:11; 14:10; 19:11–12; 20:10).

- They ensure, as best they can, that 'no one in the group is in need', selling possessions so that money can be redistributed (4:34–35), and then dealing sensibly with the administrative problems that result (6:1–7).

- They go and visit those who previously persecuted them, offering to pray for them in Jesus' name (Ananias in 9:10–19).

- Jewish believers begin to risk going into Gentile homes with Jesus' Good News, believing that, through faith in Jesus, Gentiles can truly become 'clean' and join God's new people (Peter in Cornelius' house: 10:1 – 11:18); later the apostles have a special council at which this risky new policy is confirmed and agreed (15:1–22).

- They go far from home, way beyond their comfort zone, speaking Jesus' message in remote locations north of the Taurus mountains in what is now Turkey (13:13 – 14:28).

- Through it all, when the apostles speak of Jesus, their hearers *sense the reality of Jesus* in their midst and come to faith in him (2:41); instinctively, people recognise that something of Jesus has rubbed off on 'these ordinary men of no education' – they must have been 'companions of Jesus' (4:13). In fact, what people are noticing is not just the influence of a *past Jesus* but the indwelling power of a *present Jesus*!

All this (and much else) was the outworking of Jesus' new life – his resurrection power clearly at work within those first believers by his Spirit. In other words, they did not just preach about the resurrection of Jesus, they literally lived it out. As Paul wrote later, excitedly: 'This power working in us is the same as the mighty strength which God used when he raised Christ from death' (Ephesians 1:19–20). *Jesus' followers are resurrection people* – living out the risen life of Jesus.

> *They did not just preach about the resurrection of Jesus, they literally lived it out.*

Elsewhere in the New Testament, the apostles give us three (slightly overlapping) images which help us picture this powerful reality of Jesus' risen life within us.

A. Raised to life: we have a new status and identity

The apostles teach us that we have truly been *raised to life with Christ*. The resurrection of Jesus is not a detached, isolated event. Instead, when we believe in Jesus, God includes *us* in Jesus' resurrection, by raising us from death to life. Consider these verses from Paul's teaching:

> *By our baptism ... we were buried with him and shared his death, in order that, just as Christ was raised from death by the glorious power of the Father, so also we might live a new life.*
>
> *You are to think of yourselves as dead, so far as sin is concerned, but living in fellowship with God through Christ Jesus.*
>
> ROMANS 6:4, 11

> *You were also raised with Christ through your faith in the active power of God, who raised him from death. You were at one time spiritually dead, ... but God has now brought you to life with Christ.*
>
> *You have been raised to life with Christ, so set your hearts on the things that are in heaven. For you have died, and your life is hidden with Christ in God. Your real life is Christ.*
>
> COLOSSIANS 2:12–13; 3:1, 3–4 (SEE ALSO EPHESIANS 2:5)

Believers are now truly alive in Christ. Though we were dead because of our sins, now in God's sight we are forgiven and therefore spiritually alive. This is our new status. So if God now sees us as alive, we ought also to see ourselves in this light. 'You are to think of yourselves as *living* in fellowship with God' (Romans 6:11). This is reality, not pretence. It may not feel like it, but this is a fact. Your *'real* life', as Paul says, actually *'is* Christ!' (Colossians 3:4).

This should affect the whole way in which we see our Christian lives. We are Easter people, raised to new life. Grasp this truth about your new God-given identity in Jesus and you will gain a whole new vision of what it means to follow Jesus: for, rather than being a struggle to become something you are not, the Christian life becomes instead a living out of what you already are! Be who you are! Live out your real destiny and be the person God has now made you to be!

> Rather than being a struggle to become something you are not, the Christian life becomes instead a living out of what you already are!

To help us in this, Paul encourages us to think of ourselves as 'dead, so far as sin is concerned' (Romans 6:11): our old sinful natures are 'buried' or 'put to death with Christ on his cross' (Romans 6:4, 6). If you like, our sinful natures have been mortally wounded and need to be treated as the lifeless things they truly are. Meanwhile, the positive side of this is to see our new selves as linked to the Risen Jesus. As Jesus said, our own lives are now organically dependent on his:

"... because I live, you also will live."

JOHN 14:19

We are alive in him. So our task is to stay connected to Jesus, like branches within a vine (John 15:5–7). Hence some of Paul's other instructions in Colossians: 'Since you have accepted Christ Jesus as Lord, live in union with him. Keep your roots deep in him' (Colossians 2:6–7).

The secret of the Christian life is to live *in union* with the Risen Jesus.

B. New birth: we are new people deep within

The apostles present us with the imagery of new birth. When we believe in Jesus, they teach, it is not just that we are caught up into *his* Risen life; he also places that resurrection-life into *us*! This is the 'other side of the same coin'. The Risen Jesus comes to dwell within the believer by means of his Holy Spirit (see above, chapter 3). This means several things:

- Jesus lives within us.
- Our own spirits, which were dead, come alive.
- We gain a new nature (or 'person' or 'self') deep within.
- We are 'born again' (or, better translated, 'born from above') with God's new life placed within us. For, as Jesus himself taught, 'no one can see the kingdom of God without being born again' (John 3:3).

Consider the samples from the apostles' teaching in Box 10c.

Box 10c — New life, new person

Because of his great mercy God gave us new life by raising Jesus Christ from death. ... For through the living and eternal word of God you have been born again as the children of a parent who is immortal.

1 PETER 1:3, 23

If the Spirit of God, who raised Jesus from death, lives in you, then he who raised Christ from death will also give life to your mortal bodies by the presence of his Spirit in you.

ROMANS 8:11

Anyone who is joined to Christ is a new being [or a new creation].

2 CORINTHIANS 5:17

God's ... rich and glorious secret ... is that Christ is in you.

COLOSSIANS 1:27

It is no longer I who live, but it is Christ who lives in me.

GALATIANS 2:20 (SEE ALSO PHILIPPIANS 1:21)

> *Your hearts and minds must be made completely new, and you must put on the new self, which is created in God's likeness and reveals itself in the true life that is upright and holy. ... This is the new being which God, its Creator, is constantly renewing in his own image.*
>
> EPHESIANS 4:23–24; COLOSSIANS 3:9

New life is always such an amazing thing. Hardly anyone gets bored with the idea of springtime! Few people are not moved by the sight of a newborn baby! Yet this great miracle of new life is precisely what we see taking place in the life of every believer. If we are truly Jesus' followers, then (despite how we may feel) this miracle has occurred within our lives too. In the Old Testament, the prophet Ezekiel, when picturing a valley of dry bones, saw how the bones suddenly put on flesh and became living people *at the very moment* when God breathed his Spirit upon them (Ezekiel 37:1–14). In a similar way, Jesus' Spirit can now place his life within us. We experience new birth. Although we were dead, we come to life. We are new people!

So following Jesus becomes a matter of learning to live outwards from this new Jesus-shaped person that God is developing deep within us. God has given us new natures and is creating in us a new, authentic human-ness – what Paul calls our 'new self' (our new humanity).

God has brought to life within each believer a whole new person, a new self which is fashioned 'in God's likeness'. This is now the real you – your true, God-given, individual personality. Again the message is: be true to your new self; live out who you truly are in Christ.

This means that (despite what many non-Christians think – and indeed Christians too!) the Christian life is not about trying to be good through our own efforts. It's about *living out our lives from the good, new nature that God has created in us*. God's Word still gives us clear commands about the direction in which we should go, providing, as it were, the railway lines. Yet the new, God-planted life within us also provides us with a powerful engine to travel along the track! There is a clear *pattern* laid down for the life of Jesus' followers, but there is also, gloriously, a new *power*.

> *God has brought to life within each believer a whole new person, a new self which is fashioned 'in God's likeness'.*

So, as new people, our chief aim is simply to let the new life of Jesus within us shine through.

C. Life in the Spirit: we have a new power

The apostles describe this new life as the presence within us of Jesus' *Spirit*. When asked how exactly the Risen Jesus can live within us, they would answer that it is by means of the Holy Spirit. We saw this above (in chapter 3), but now we must focus more on how this can be lived out in practice. For the apostles teach us that, if we are to live Jesus' risen life, we must 'live according to the Spirit' (Romans 8:4). This is the normal Christian life, each and every day. But what does this look like?

We saw above how Jesus wanted his life within us to 'bear much fruit' (John 15:5). Paul later gives us a list of this fruit, which significantly he calls the 'fruit of the Spirit'. He focuses on nine key items: 'love, joy, peace, patience, kindness, goodness, faithfulness, humility, and self-control' (Galatians 5:22–23).

This list may seem daunting – after all, these words describe *Jesus'* character far better than they describe *ours*! But that's precisely the point: that same *Jesus is now living in us by his Spirit* and will produce these fruits in our lives – if we let his Spirit do so. So Paul goes on:

> Let the Spirit direct your lives. ... The Spirit has given us life;
> he must also control our lives.
>
> GALATIANS 5:16, 25

We are to be controlled, led, and directed by the Spirit.

To be sure, the production of this fruit may take time and cannot be rushed. Moreover, because of our continuing sinfulness, we will often hinder the Spirit's work, indeed grieve him and make him 'sad' (Ephesians 4:30). Yet, day by day, there is the opportunity to let the Spirit work. This is the way to bear fruit in following Jesus.

This special resource – the gift of Jesus' Spirit within us – should therefore encourage us every time we hear the apostles giving us instructions and commands about how we should live (see Box 10d).

Box 10d — Life in the Spirit: holiness

Be holy in all that you do, just as God who called you is holy. ... Rid yourselves ... of all evil; no more lying or hypocrisy or jealousy or insulting language.

1 Peter 1:15; 2:1

You must clothe yourselves with compassion, kindness, humility, gentleness, and patience. Be tolerant with one another and forgive one another ... just as the Lord has forgiven you. And to all these qualities add love.

Colossians 3:12–14

Fill your minds with those things that are good and that deserve praise: things that are true, noble, right, pure, lovely, and honourable.

Philippians 4:8

Try to be at peace with everyone, and try to live a holy life, because no one will see the Lord without it.

Hebrews 12:14

Love must be completely sincere. ... Let your hope keep you joyful, be patient in your troubles, and pray at all times. Share your belongings with your needy fellow-Christians, and open your homes to strangers.

Ask God to bless those who persecute you. ... Do everything possible on your part to live in peace with everybody. Never take revenge, my friends. ... Do not let evil defeat you; instead conquer evil with good.

Romans 12:9, 12–14, 18–19, 21

For other New Testament passages on Christian lifestyle, see also Ephesians 4:17 – 6:9; 1 Thessalonians 5:12–22; 1 Peter 4; 1 John 3.

These commands reflect the apostles' brilliant vision for Christian living: life lived in the power of the Spirit. Note their concern for personal holiness; note their vision for building Christian communities; note too their wider vision for showing forth God's kingdom in the world. As Paul says elsewhere, 'we should do good to *everyone*' (Galatians 6:10).

This last point makes plain that this wider, less self-absorbed focus is all part of following Jesus. As we saw, those first believers in Acts had a vision for bringing not just their own lives as individuals – indeed not just their small congregations – but the *whole world* under the saving rule of King Jesus. They were, in Jesus' words, to be 'like salt for the whole human race' (Matthew 5:13), being closely stuck into the world with all its disease and sickness, yet always acting as the agents of new life and healing. So the apostles want us to bring the power of Jesus' life into every situation we meet, transforming it with his light and love.

> *Bring the power of Jesus' life into every situation, transforming it with his light and love.*

It's a daunting challenge and we need to heed their words, submitting our sinful wills obediently to God's word as spoken through them. That word was inspired by the very Spirit who now lives within us. So the important point is this: God has given us a powerful resource that can enable us to live out this spectacular vision for life. In other words, the *Spirit of Jesus given to us* is to bring about the *lifestyle of Jesus in us*. The Spirit indeed is our 'Helper' (John 14:16); the Spirit who commands is also the Spirit that enables. We have been given *principles to observe* but also the *power to obey*.

This spiritual reality underlies everything else the New Testament teaches us about how we should now live for God. New Testament commands, if always demanding, are also *enticing expressions of what God's new life in us can bring about*; they are invitations to walk in his way and in his God-given strength. We are called to live a new lifestyle,

> *We have been given principles to observe but also the power to obey.*

but first we are given a new life! In other words, we don't need to 'get a life' – we already have it!

So the tenth building-block in following Jesus is to *live his life*. At first sight, it sounds so daunting. Yet we have learnt that the Risen Jesus is living within us by his Spirit. Living Jesus' life, then, turns out to mean letting Jesus live his life through us. It all becomes possible because, in him, we are truly new persons, raised to new life.

The question is: will we let Jesus live his risen life through us?

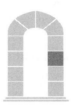

Building-block 10

Live His Life
– You Are a New Person!

Resist His Enemy

> Peter said to them, "Each one of you must turn away from your sins and be ... forgiven." And with many other words he urged them, saying, "Save yourselves from the punishment coming on this wicked people!"

ACTS 2:38, 40

Living for Jesus is not all plain sailing. There may be new resources, as we have seen, but there is also some new opposition. Peter names quite clearly the issue of human sins and wickedness. And those first followers of Jesus soon discovered that evil remained a powerful reality – even in the life of a Spirit-empowered community. Hence, for example, Luke's honest account of the way one couple, Ananias and Sapphira, told lies about their finances (Acts 5:1–11). The coming of the Holy Spirit clearly did not bring about a perfect, sinless church – nor has it ever resulted in a single sin-free 'saint'!

The apostles' teaching will therefore have included, not just a positive portrait of how Jesus' followers should live, but also a more negative message, warning them about those things they must firmly resist. If they must repent of their sins at the very start of their Christian lives, they must continue to resist sin throughout their lives. After all, Jesus himself had clearly taught that following him would be tough: "Anyone who wants to come with me must forget self, take up their cross every day, and follow me" (Luke 9:23). And he was clear that human beings have a battle on their hands in combating the evil in their lives:

> For from the inside, from a person's heart, come the evil ideas which lead him to do immoral things, to rob, kill, commit adultery, be greedy, and do all sorts of evil things: deceit, indecency, jealousy, slander, pride, and folly...

MARK 7:21–22

So being his follower will always mean turning against the tide, going upstream, resisting evil and sometimes dealing severely with our own desires and agendas. Yes, it is the way of new life and resurrection, but it is also the way of the cross, death and self-denial.

The eleventh building-block in the Christian life, then, is this: to be on our guard against anything that is opposed to Jesus; to *resist his 'enemy'* that is anything that is inimical (or contrary) to his truth, his light or his love. This will involve a frank recognition of the reality and power of evil – both in ourselves and in the world.

Jesus' resurrection is a sure pledge from God that he himself is actively involved in the real world, himself bringing good out of evil, and life out of death. Moreover, Jesus' ascension is a sure sign that God fully vindicated Jesus, completely endorsing all his goodness, and so is totally opposed to all that is evil. Evidently, if *we* are going to be vindicated by God in any way, then we will need to side firmly and squarely with Jesus. If Jesus is the embodiment of light, we will need to turn our backs on darkness.

Interestingly, this theme is hinted at right there on that first day of Pentecost. Quoting some Old Testament words (which, intriguingly, Jesus had earlier applied to himself: Mark 12:35–37), Peter portrays God the Father as now effectively saying to Jesus: "Sit here at my right until I put your enemies as a footstool under your feet" (Psalm 110:1 in Acts 2:34–35). Evidently, from Jesus' ascension onwards, human history is going to be an extended period in which God brings Jesus' enemies to be under his feet. Paul later develops this idea, applying this same text to Christ's victory over our greatest enemy, namely death itself (1 Corinthians 15:27). This gives us an indication that the 'enemies' in view here are not so much individual human enemies, but rather humanity's big, long-term Enemies: sin, evil, death and any spiritual forces of darkness.

> If Jesus is the embodiment of light, we will need to turn our backs on darkness.

We also learn from Peter's words that God is opposed to anything which stands in the way of Jesus and his kingdom and is working towards that day when any such opposition to King Jesus is overthrown. Will we turn our backs resolutely on these things in our lives? Will we resist evil in all its forms for Jesus' sake?

Recognising the real enemy

Is there a danger that *we ourselves* could ever be classed as God's enemies? There is. Scripture teaches, 'In our natural condition we ... were destined to suffer God's anger' (Ephesians 2:3). This means that, until we repent of our own evil and disobedience, we are under God's judgement and in need of being reconciled to him. Yet, through the gospel, God converts his former enemies into his friends:

> *We were God's enemies, but he made us his friends through the death of his Son.*
>
> ROMANS 5:10

The cross becomes the place where our own animosity towards God is dissolved and our status as his enemies removed. 'God was making the whole human race his friends through Christ and did not keep an account of their sins' (2 Corinthians 5:19).

So the Good News, as some of Peter's hearers found out, is that those who respond to Jesus by faith are thereby *automatically* removed from being counted as God's enemies. If we have come under the rule of King Jesus, then we have been 'rescued ... from the power of darkness' and brought into 'the kingdom of his dear Son' (Colossians 1:13).

Great! But now we need to resist that power of darkness. How do we do this? Despite what some extremists might be tempted to think, such resistance will *never* involve Jesus' followers taking God's law into their own hands and aiming to harm (or even kill) those whom *they* judge to be God's enemies. Jesus and the apostles show us clearly that such a radical response is entirely inappropriate.

In his Sermon on the Mount, Jesus spoke out against murder – indeed even against thoughts of anger (Matthew 5:21–22). Instead, he encouraged his followers to love their enemies and pray for those who persecuted them (Matthew 5:44) – something he acted out himself when being nailed to the cross, saying, "Father, forgive them!" (Luke 23:34). Nor do we see the apostles taking up weapons. 'Instead,' writes Paul, 'as the scripture says: "If your enemies are hungry, feed them"' (Romans 12:20). Christians should never 'take revenge' (12:19). On the contrary, as Peter says in his letter, we should be following in the steps of Jesus: 'When he was insulted, he did not answer back with an insult; when he suffered, he did not threaten, but placed his hopes in God, the righteous Judge' (1 Peter 2:23). So, clearly, no physical attacks are ever allowed on a Christian's personal enemies. It is far too easy to assume, wrongly, that *our* enemy is automatically *God's* enemy. Such thinking is highly dangerous; as James says,

> Human anger does not achieve God's righteous purpose.
> JAMES 1:20

So, if this is the case, which 'enemy' of Jesus *should* we be fighting? The chilling response is this: the chief enemy of Jesus is sin, and the chief place where we should be resisting this enemy is not in other people, but in *our own lives*. Most of the time, we need look no further! After all, Jesus warned us: "Do not judge others. ... Why do you look at the speck in your brother's eye, and pay no attention to the log in your own eye?" (Matthew 7:1, 3). Or we might say, we must always be first looking in the mirror, not only through the window. Jesus' chief enemy is *within* – within *us*!

In chapter 2 we saw how seriously the Bible speaks of sin. This deadly disease (that makes us choose our own way, worshipping our own selves rather than God) is within us all, and it can only be cured by the cross of Jesus – where the penalty for sin was borne and evil in all its forms was decisively conquered. Yet now we notice this further solemn reality. Although, as Jesus' followers, we recognise this account of sin (and so should be coming always to Jesus' cross in repentance, asking for his forgiveness), *we continue to be deeply sinful*. Though forgiven by God, we are not perfect. As Martin Luther (1483 -1546) famously observed, we may be declared 'righteous' in God's sight (or 'put right' with him), yet at the same time we remain sinners: we are 'simultaneously forgiven and sinful' (in his Latin phrase: *simul justus ac peccator*).

It is true that a few interpreters have thought some New Testament verses encourage a belief in the possibility of sinless perfection*. Most of us, however, know only too well that we are not perfect! The truth of our ongoing sinfulness is all too obvious to us – sometimes painfully so. Yet, even if obvious, this still remains a serious state of affairs. God does not stop seeing sin as his enemy,

> Jesus' chief enemy is *within* – within *us*!

just because the person in whom it is present is now a believer. Sin remains evil, a blot on his good creation. The believer needs to fight it, to resist it and (when necessary) to repent. This is made clear in many baptism services (see Appendix C): new believers not only renounce evil, but are often commissioned to be Christ's 'faithful soldier and servant' and to 'fight valiantly under the banner of Christ against sin, the world, and the Devil*'. This is a realistic reminder of what it means to be a follower of Jesus — it's a lifelong battle against evil, in all its forms.

> God does not stop seeing sin as his enemy, just because the person in whom it is present is now a believer.

Sin, the world, and the Devil

This threefold description of evil will be a useful one as we now look in some more detail at the apostles' teaching on this 'enemy' of Jesus that we must resist.

Sin

In some earlier baptismal services, those being baptised were asked to renounce 'the world, the flesh, and the Devil'. Because the word 'flesh'* sounds quite strange to our ears, this has now been rendered instead by the word 'sin'. But what was 'flesh' trying to convey? It was included in baptism services because the apostles used this particular term (*sarx* in Greek) to describe what we might now call our sinful 'human nature' – that is, our innate human tendency to be self-centred, rather than God-centred. Let's hear Paul's explanation of this key term in Galatians:

> What I say is this: let the Spirit direct your lives, and you will not satisfy the desires of the human nature. For what our human nature wants is opposed to what the Spirit wants, and what the Spirit wants is opposed to what our human nature wants. These two are enemies, and this means that you cannot do what you want to do. ...
>
> What human nature does is quite plain: it shows itself in immoral, filthy, and indecent actions; in worship of idols and witchcraft. People become enemies and they fight;

*they become jealous, angry, and ambitious. They separate
into parties and groups; they are envious, get drunk, have
orgies, and do other things like these. I warn you now as I
have before: those who do these things will not possess the
kingdom of God.*

GALATIANS 5:16–17, 19–21

For Paul, believers are in a battle. Or, you might say, there's a battle
going on *in them*. He speaks of God's Spirit being within us, but so too
is our old human nature (our *sarx*) — and these two, says Paul 'are
enemies'! We will never get very far in the Christian life if we do not
come to terms with this awkward fact. For, although Jesus
has indeed placed his new life within us by his Spirit, this
new life will soon be under attack. In the imagery of one
of his parables, we may have received the 'good seed' into
the soil of our lives, but the soil still produces weeds (Mark 4:13–20).
We have been given a 'new self', a new Christ-like nature (see above,
chapter 10), but our old sinful nature is also alive and kicking. In other
words, there is a continual tension within each of us between the flesh
and the Spirit, and this tension will be with us till the day we die. There
are two opposing principles at work within us. We are in for a long-
haul fight.

> There are two
> opposing principles at
> work within us.

Box 11 — The apostles' teaching about sinful behaviour

*You must put to death ... the earthly desires at work in you, such as
sexual immorality, indecency, lust, evil passions and greed. ...
    You must get rid of all these things: anger, passion, and hateful
feelings. No insults or obscene talk must ever come from your lips.
Do not lie to one another, for you have taken off the old self with its
habits and have put on the new self.*

COLOSSIANS 3:5, 8–9

*Rid yourselves ... of all evil: no more lying or hypocrisy or jealousy
or insulting language. ...
    Do not give in to bodily passions, which are always at war against
the soul. ... From now on, then, you must live the rest of your earthly
lives controlled by God's will and not by human desires which lead*

to indecency, lust, drunkenness, orgies, drinking parties, and the disgusting worship of idols.

1 PETER 2:1, 11; 4:2

Marriage is to be honoured by all, and husbands and wives must be faithful to each other. God will judge those who are immoral and those who commit adultery. ... Keep your lives free from the love of money.

HEBREWS 13:4–5

Everyone must be quick to listen, but ... slow to become angry. ... So get rid of every filthy habit and all wicked conduct. Submit to God and accept the word that he plants in your hearts, which is able to save you.

JAMES 1:19, 21

This conviction about our sinful human natures (the flesh) and of their continuing power in believers' lives undergirds the apostles' many strong warnings about sin (as seen in Box 11). These are tough words, giving us a flavour of the New Testament's moral challenge. The apostles knew they had to be specific about sin, to name particular sins, and to warn Jesus' followers to resist these things. We must heed their challenge.

The world

In biblical thought, however, 'sin' does not simply refer to the evil that exists within our own person (the flesh). It also describes the whole web of corruption and evil in human society – what the apostle John calls the 'world':

Do not love the world or anything that belongs to the world. If you love the world, you do not love the Father. Everything that belongs to the world – what the sinful self desires, what people see and want, and everything in this world that people are so proud of – none of this comes from the Father; it all comes from the world. The world and everything in it that people desire is passing away; but those who do the will of God live for ever.

1 JOHN 2:15–17

John's use of the word 'world' helps us realise the scale of the problem. Sin affects everyone, John is saying, and it has led to a *whole way of life* that is contrary to God's will. The 'world' thus becomes, for John, the place that stands opposed to God. Yes, God loves the created world and human life – indeed 'God loved the world so much that he gave his only Son' (John 3:16) – but in another sense the 'world' must be viewed negatively, referring to human beings in their collective hostility towards God. It is the world in *this* sense that John calls us to renounce – hence his focus on people's desires and pride. Jesus' followers must be driven by a different desire (for God) and must set their hearts and goals in a different place. We are not to 'love the world' but 'the Father'.

Jesus himself had prayed for his followers not to 'belong to the world' (John 17:14–16). Similarly, Paul describes how believers should conduct their lives:

> *Do not conform yourselves to the standards of this world.*
> ROMANS 12:2

It is not too hard to think what the values and standards of the world are: selfish materialism, ambition, envy, strife, sexual licence, etc. We are to get wise, acknowledging that this is the way the 'world' operates, choosing not to belong to it, and then cutting a different way through life. As James says: 'Don't you know that to be the world's friend means to be God's enemy?' (James 4:4).

The Devil

There is more. We are not just fighting against our own inner desires or the pressure of an unbelieving world. We are also up against a personal force of evil, called in Scripture by different names: the 'Evil One' (Matthew 6:13), the 'accuser' (Revelation 12:10 NIV), the 'evil god of this world' (2 Corinthians 4:4), but especially Satan* (meaning the 'adversary') and the Devil* (the 'slanderer').

Jesus' ministry reveals this surprising truth – that the Devil is a real spiritual being. Having been himself tested by the Devil at the start of his ministry, Jesus later warns Peter that Satan is luring him away from the truth; on another occasion, he celebrates his followers' success in terms of Satan falling 'like lightning', and views his own exorcisms as clear signs that Satan is like a captive 'strong man' who is having his house 'plundered'. Indeed, Satan is being 'driven out' by the arrival of Jesus, and Jesus' death is the moment when the 'ruler of this world' is roundly defeated (for references see the glossary under 'Devil'). Here is Jesus' blunt summary about the one we are dealing with:

> *"From the very beginning he was a murderer and has never been on the side of truth, because there is no truth in him. When he tells a lie, he is only doing what is natural to him, because he is a liar and the father of lies."*

JOHN 8:44

The apostles teach the same, describing Satan as eternally sinful, a master of 'disguise' and someone who blinds people to Jesus' truth. They warn us consistently to be on our guard against him (for references, again see the glossary). In one passage, Paul expressly encourages us to see ourselves as soldiers fighting against the 'wicked spiritual forces in the heavenly world' and standing against 'the Devil's evil tricks'. We are to put on all 'God's armour' — for example, 'truth as a belt', 'faith as a shield' (Ephesians 6:10–14). In other words, Jesus' followers are in a spiritual battle. The Evil One stands opposed to Jesus and is therefore our enemy too.

Jesus' followers are in a spiritual battle.

This is not meant to frighten us. Through his cross, Jesus 'freed himself from the power' of the Devil and dealt him a killer blow (Colossians 2:15); moreover, Jesus promises that no one will be able to 'snatch away' his followers from his loving care (John 10:28). Even so, we should not minimise Satan's power. Many things in the world can be explained only by reference to the active involvement of the Evil One. We are not therefore to be ignorant of his strategies. These include things such as temptation and deception. And his influence can be seen not just in individual lives but also corporately — in the way that human institutions, societies and indeed nations so easily veer towards injustice, oppression and selfishness.

The Evil One especially loves to 'accuse' believers, making us feel guilty. If so, we must come back to the cross, and so find again the truth of our being forgiven and accepted by God. In this and other ways, Jesus' followers must recognise the Evil One and be ready to resist him — not in our own strength, but through the powerful blood of Jesus. Put on God's armour and you will be able to stand firm; or, as James succinctly puts it:

> Resist the Devil, and he will run away from you.
>
> JAMES 4:7

Practical strategies

Sin, then, is a complex reality. When trying to explain the cause of a particular evil, we may need to use a combination of each of these three explanations from the Bible (the flesh, the world, and the Devil) — something we see helpfully explored in the letter of James (see James 1:14–15; 3:14–15; 4:4). Understanding this will help us as we seek to resist the enemy of sin in our own lives. Yes, we must always accept responsibility for our own thoughts and actions. Yet becoming aware — both of the pressures coming to us from the world and of the real intervention of the Evil One — can help us see other factors which are genuinely at work. Indeed, sometimes temptation can lose its grip over us the very moment we recognise in it the wily hand of the Evil One; at that point, echoing Jesus' words, we can say with direct confidence, "Get away from me, Satan!" (Mark 8:33).

Here are some further biblical tips for resisting the enemy of sin in our lives and the lure of temptation:

1. Remember you are not alone

Others have faced the same temptation before. Paul writes: 'Every test that you have experienced is the kind that normally comes to people'. Yet he then adds a promise: 'God will give you the strength to endure the test, and so provide you with a way out' (1 Corinthians 10:13). Even more importantly, we are not alone because Jesus himself has faced these temptations:

> Jesus ... is not one who cannot feel sympathy for our weaknesses. On the contrary, we have a High Priest who was tempted in every way that we are, but did not sin.
>
> HEBREWS 4:15

2. Reckon your old natures as dead in God's sight

Here is a profound spiritual mystery: it never feels true that our old natures are dead, but they are. We saw above (chapter 10) how Jesus' followers have been made alive in Christ and given a *new* nature (or 'being'). However, the converse is true too: 'our *old* being has been put to death with Christ on his cross; ... you are to think of yourselves as dead, so far as sin is concerned' (Romans 6:6, 11). This means we should stop paying attention to our sinful nature (even though it continues to operate within us daily). Instead, we are to see it as effectively nailed to the cross: 'those who belong to Christ Jesus have put to death their human nature [the flesh] with all its passions and desires' (Galatians 5:24). Not for nothing does Jesus command his followers to 'take up their cross *every day*' (Luke 9:23). In this way, we can start operating from our new selves – given us in Christ – and draw strength from our union with Jesus.

3. Feed your mind and imagination on God's truth

Many believers live depressed lives because they believe lies: they imagine, for example, that they are worthless, unable to be forgiven, always on their own, unable to hear God or speak with him. Instead, we are to feed on the truth of God's word, replacing such lies with the liberating truths of Scripture. Jesus himself, when tempted, simply responded by standing firmly on biblical truth: "The scripture says ..." (see Matthew 4:4–10). And Paul, in encouraging us to put on God's armour (above), begins by having us put on 'truth' as a belt. Moreover, since much temptation begins in our imaginations, he advises us to replace with more positive thoughts any evil ideas or images that begin to linger there:

> Fill your minds with things that are true, noble, right, pure, lovely, and honourable.

PHILIPPIANS 4:8

'So, let us keep our eyes fixed on Jesus' (Hebrews 12:2), worshipping him and placing him at the centre of our lives. If we do, the grip of sin will lose much of its power.

4. Remove yourself from situations, if necessary

In the Old Testament, there is a memorable example of this, when Joseph flees from the seductive advances of Potiphar's wife (Genesis 39:12). This is not a sign of weakness but a starkly practical decision. Sometimes this decision is made in advance ("I won't go there!"); sometimes it can only be made once we find ourselves in a situation where remaining true to Jesus is going to be difficult ("It's time to leave!"). The New Testament simply uses the plain language of avoidance: 'avoid immorality', 'avoid the passions of youth' (1 Corinthians 6:18; 2 Timothy 2:22).

5. Be disciplined with yourself

Our bodies can develop instincts that go in the direction of the 'flesh' but, as we give ourselves to delight in God and let the Spirit work his way outwards through our lives, *these instincts can be retrained* in the direction of Jesus' kingdom. Hence Paul's call to us to 'put to death' our sinful actions by the Spirit (Romans 8:13); hence too his own disciplined (even athletic) approach to his own body (1 Corinthians 9:27). Retraining our instincts may require planned effort and the use of such godly disciplines as study, solitude, silence and worship.

> *Retraining our instincts may require planned effort and the use of such godly disciplines as study, solitude, silence and worship.*

6. Keep short accounts with God

In any relationship it's good to prevent grievances building up by ensuring that forgiveness is sought as soon as possible. We are to settle disputes 'while there is time', warns Jesus (Matthew 5:25). The same is true with God. If we fail to claim his forgiveness each day, we may soon find we have a vague sense of guilt and that God seems strangely far away. It then gets more difficult to come back to him and, once in this position, we are very prone to falling yet further. Here's a downward spiral which (to mix one's metaphors!) it is worth 'nipping in the bud'.

7. Don't always stay on the back foot

There will be times when it is appropriate to challenge evils in the wider society in Jesus' name, promoting God's righteousness and the cause of his justice. Jesus proclaimed that God was king and he himself took that challenge to the rulers of his day and to the heart of his own nation. We need to do the same – defending the rights of those unable to defend themselves from predators in the ocean of life, and announcing in practice that evil shall not have the last word in Jesus' world. It is always good to demonstrate that the 'powers' at work in the world have met their match in Jesus and to show people that there is another way of being human – the way of love. So, even if the focus of this present chapter has necessarily been on our own individual lives, this should not cause us to forget the big concerns of the Bible for righteousness in human society, and for bringing in the values of that alternative kingdom, the kingdom of God. Thus international peace, fair trade, the relief of poverty – these are all on God's heart, and those who name Jesus as king will need to contend for these things in whatever quarter, humbly but courageously. Where there is suffering, bring Christ's compassion; but, where there is evil, confront it.

> *It is always good to demonstrate that the 'powers' at work in the world have met their match in Jesus.*

Conclusion

> *Take your part ... as a loyal soldier of Christ Jesus.*
>
> 2 TIMOTHY 2:3

The apostles saw the Christian life as a kind of warfare; they clearly taught that, if we are going to be Jesus' followers, we will need to be ready to fight in this spiritual battle. So we are going to need to get wise about the real enemy and to learn how to use the weapons we have been given: 'The weapons we use in our fight are not the world's weapons but God's powerful weapons' and they are to be used in order to 'take every thought captive and make it obey Christ' (2 Corinthians 10:4–5). There's the vision – to see evil made captive to Christ, and thus to see the enemies of Jesus come at last under his feet (Acts 2:35).

　　The eleventh building-block is to *resist his enemy*; and we have seen that Jesus' 'enemy' is anything that is evil – what the Bible calls 'sin' in all its many forms. As a result, we are to fight this wherever we find it — especially in ourselves and in our own old natures, but also in human society.

As individuals, we are to put on God's special armour and resist the Evil One (see Ephesians 6:10–18). Yet we are also to take courage from the fact that, ultimately, the victory is assured. In the imagery of Revelation, Jesus is the conqueror and his people are victorious: the 'great accuser' is overthrown, and evil is removed far from God's people (Revelation 21:8; see further below chapter 12). So, although in this life the battle will never be over (and we ourselves will remain far from perfect), we can take heart: we are on the winning side! "The world will make you suffer," Jesus said. "But be brave! I have defeated the world!" (John 16:33).

We are therefore to press on towards this victory through the power of the cross. For this is where Jesus overcame all our sins and where the 'rulers of this world' were defeated (1 Corinthians 2:8; Colossians 2:15). We keep on coming back to the cross — the place where the Christian life begins and the place where it must always continue.

The question is: are we ready to be soldiers of the cross, playing our part in the Lord's true army? Will we renounce all evil, knowing that it is the enemy of Jesus? Human sin is what caused him to die, and the whole purpose of his coming was 'to destroy what the Devil had done' (1 John 3:8). But the cross was also the place where sin — the flesh, the world, the Devil — was publicly humiliated and defeated. So his followers must fight.

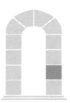

Building-block 11

Resist His Enemy
– All Evil was Defeated on the Cross!

12

Trust Him for the Future

"God raised Jesus from death, setting him free from its power. ...
David said about him: 'You will not allow your faithful servant to
rot in the grave; ... your presence will fill me with joy.'"

ACTS 2:24–25, 27–28

One of the most striking things about the opening chapters of Acts is the upsurge of confidence and hope that is suddenly hitting the world. The apostles and those first believers are marked by a new, daring approach to life. A few days earlier, they had been full of fear, meeting in secret (John 20:19); the Emmaus disciples had been 'sad' and talking about their dashed hopes (Luke 24:17, 21); indeed Peter had denied Jesus three times (Luke 22:54–62). But now, what a contrast! Throughout Acts 2 – 7 we see first Peter, next John, and then all the believers, speaking out boldly in Jesus' name, risking arrest, and being ready to suffer for Jesus' sake. What can explain this dramatic change – from cowardice into courage, from despair into hope?

Answer: the resurrection of Jesus and the gift of his Spirit. These two great events have convinced them that their God is powerful and active, and have also given them a glimpse into the future. In particular, by looking at Jesus' resurrection, they can see how death has not been able to 'hold him prisoner' (2:24); this surely means that, for them too as believers, physical death will not be the final end – there will be resurrection life beyond the grave. Again, looking at Jesus' resurrection, they also begin to realise that they have probably not seen the last of Jesus! This eternal person, now seated for a while at God's right-hand side, will one day be back. Thus, a few days later, Peter asserts that this Jesus "must remain in heaven", but only "until the time comes for all things to be made new" (3:21). That's their vision: through the resurrection, God has done a bright, new thing, which is a sure sign that, when Jesus returns, he will one day make all things new. It's enough to fill them with undaunted confidence and with an assured hope.

So, as we give ourselves to the apostles' teaching, a key part of this will be to learn from them about what the future holds, now that Jesus has been raised from the dead. How did they see the future unfolding — for Jesus, for believers, indeed for the world? And in our day, when so many find life meaningless, hopeless and a recipe for despair, what can the apostles teach us that will bring into our lives a sure basis for optimism and hope?

Their writings in the New Testament (as can be seen in Box 12a) turn out to be shot through with great expectations; they pulsate with bright colours and dynamic energy. Someone has estimated that at least one in 20 verses makes some specific reference to this glorious hope. Evidently, the Christian Good News, unlike most news stories, has something very clear to say about the future.

How is this so? Because the future has been anchored in a solid event in past human history: Jesus' resurrection. In the Bible, the word translated 'hope' (despite the way this word is sometimes used in English) does not mean some vague, wishful thinking; rather, it is an *attitude built on something fixed, concrete and reliable*. If you like, God, through the resurrection, has revealed his future in seed-form — in outline. In the midst of human history, God has done something which speaks loud and clear about the *end* of human history. We now know the goal that he has for the future, because of what he has revealed of that future *in the past*.

> The future has been anchored in a solid event in past human history: Jesus' resurrection.

In that sense, we are to go 'back to the future'! Or, to use a biblical image, Jesus' resurrection is the 'first fruits' of a harvest still to come – a sure sign of what God will do again in the future, both for individuals and for the world. It is, in other words, his 'first instalment' – a down payment on what he pledges will be the future of the world.

As believers in Jesus, then, we are to be infused with a strong dose of hope – a sense that the 'best is yet to be'. Sometimes life is indeed hard: the suffering in our world is great, and the battle against evil long and tiresome. But there is a light at the end of the tunnel! There is solid ground on which we can stand.

So the twelfth and final building-block in following Jesus today is to be grounded in hope – to listen carefully to what his apostles teach us about the future and then to *trust him for that future*. As we now listen to the apostles as they explain and describe this hope, we will note what they say about God's plans for the world and for believers under three headings: renewal for the world, reunion with Jesus, and resurrection for the believer.

Box 12a – The apostles' teaching: hope for the future

God gave us new life by raising Jesus Christ from death. This fills us with a living hope, and so we look forward to possessing the rich blessings that God keeps for his people. He keeps them for you in heaven, where they cannot decay or spoil or fade away. ... So then ... set your hope completely on the blessing which will be given you when Jesus Christ is revealed.

1 PETER 1:3–5, 13

We know that when Christ appears, we shall be like him. ... Everyone who has this hope in Christ keeps himself pure, just as Christ is pure.

1 JOHN 3:2–3

To have faith is to be sure of the things we hope for.

HEBREW 11:1

If Christ has not been raised from death, then we have nothing to preach. ... It would also mean that the believers in Christ who have died are lost. ... But the truth is that Christ has been raised from death, as the guarantee that those who sleep in death will also be raised. ...

When you sow a seed in the ground, it does not sprout to life unless it dies. And what you sow is a bare seed, ... not the full-bodied plant that will later grow up. ...

This is how it will be when the dead are raised to life. When the body is buried, ... it is ugly and weak; when raised, it will be beautiful and strong. When buried, it is physical body; when raised, it will be a spiritual body. ...

For when the trumpet sounds, the dead will be raised, never to die again, and we shall all be changed. ... Then the scripture will come true: 'Death is destroyed; victory is complete!'

1 CORINTHIANS 15:14, 18, 20, 36–37, 42–44, 51–52, 54

Then I saw a new heaven and a new earth. The first heaven and the first earth disappeared, and the sea vanished. And I saw the Holy City, the new Jerusalem, coming down out of heaven from God, prepared and ready, like a bride dressed to meet her husband. I heard a loud voice speaking from the throne: "Now God's home is with human beings! He will live with them, and they shall be his people. God himself will be with them, and he will be their God. He will wipe away all tears from their eyes. There will be no more death, no more grief or crying or pain. The old things have disappeared."

Then the one who sits on the throne said, "And now I make all things new!"

REVELATION 21:1–5

For other related passages, see 1 Corinthians 13:13; Ephesians 1:18; 1 Peter 1:3–9; 3:15 and Colossians 1:3–5.

Renewal for the world

This first theme may come as something of a shock. In the light of what we have just said, it might be imagined that the Christian message is all about some place else – heaven, not earth. But in fact, the Bible is an earthy book, and biblical hope, in both Old and New Testaments, is far more down to earth. 'The world and all that is in it belongs to the LORD' (Psalm 24:1). So, although evil has come into the world, there is the strong hope that this world 'will be as full of knowledge of the LORD as the seas are full of water' (Isaiah 11:9). Creation has been damaged, but God will bring about a renewed creation. So, as believers, our individual hopes are to be set within this much larger context of God's agenda for the renewal of his world.

We see Paul making exactly this point in Romans 8:

I consider that what we suffer at this present time cannot be compared at all with the glory that is going to be revealed to us. All of creation waits with eager longing for God to reveal his children. For creation was condemned to lose its purpose, not of its own will, but because God willed it to be so. Yet there was the hope that creation itself would one day be set free from its slavery to decay and would share the glorious freedom of the children of God. For we know that up to the present time all of creation groans with pain, like the pain of childbirth. But it is not just creation alone which groans: we who have the Spirit as the first of God's gifts also groan within ourselves, as we wait for God to make us his children and set our whole being free.

ROMANS 8:18–23

According to Paul, God is going to share his glory with his own people; believers in Jesus (those who already have the 'first fruits' of God's Spirit) will be revealed as his true children. Yet on that day, *creation too will be blessed*. Creation has experienced a 'slavery to decay'; it groans like a woman in childbirth; but these are the labour pains before a new age, a new creation. This is our hope, but this is also creation's 'hope'. So, whenever we see painful things in our world, such as decay and death, we are yet to have confidence through the resurrection that *this is not God's last word on the subject*. If human beings will find their ultimate renewal through Jesus and the Spirit, so too will creation itself.

God, then, is moving the old creation through to a glorious new creation. This conviction can help us view many things in a whole new way:

- We can see our *physical world* not as something to be abused (because it might one day be discarded), but rather as something to be nurtured and cared for (because God is going to redeem it or 'set it free').
- We can sense that the whole process of *human history* is something through which God is mysteriously at work.
- We can see our own *individual human lives*, not as something to be dismissed (before we get on and do the real thing – in heaven!) but as something valuable in their own right – as the theatre of God's redeeming work.

The basis for this new perspective on human life and the created world is, again, the resurrection of Jesus. It is precisely when we see God *not discarding Jesus' corpse but rather transforming it and renewing it as a physical body*, that we realise God is not in the business of discarding his broken, bruised world; rather he has the power and purpose to renew it with his healing love. In contrast to many sub-Christian views, which are often dualist*, the resurrection body of Jesus makes abundantly clear that *physical matter is not inherently evil; it is only sin and suffering that are evil.* One day, this physical world will see these ugly intrusions on God's good creation visibly removed once and for all. The resurrection of Jesus is a sure sign of God's plan to renew the world; it is his pledge to his decaying *old* creation that he is bringing in his transformed *new* creation.

> The resurrection of Jesus is a sure sign of God's plan to renew the world; it is his pledge to his decaying *old* creation that he is bringing in his transformed *new* creation.

The New Testament closes with the great picture book of Revelation (see the extract in Box 12a). As the last book in the Bible, it reworks the imagery used in the Bible's very first book (Genesis). Through Jesus, God has taken history from the old first creation (described in Genesis 1 – 2) to a new, more glorious creation. When read carefully, its final vision of God's future (in Revelation 21) does not speak of our created world being destroyed, but rather of God renewing it – taking the old and making everything new:

> Then the one who sits on the throne said, "And now I am making all things new!"
>
> REVELATION 21:5

Thus we should understand the 'new earth' described here in the sense of a *re-newed* earth. On that day, the world will be truly redeemed and the old creation brought through into a glorious new creation. Note too that the Christian hope is clearly not so much that we go to heaven; rather it is that heaven now comes to us! This is God's 'earthy' plan for the renewal of his created world.

Reunion with Jesus

The resurrection also points us forward to an incredible truth about Jesus himself: not just that he is both 'Lord and Messiah' (Acts 2:36), but that he is coming back! From his resurrection, the apostles could deduce that Jesus was an eternal person who would never die again (see chapter 1 above). Moreover, from his ascension into heaven, they would learn that he was now living in God's nearer presence. This, then, clearly meant that, somehow or other, there would be an opportunity to meet him again. Although he had departed from them, this was clearly *not* the end of the story!

This is precisely what the angels told the apostles at the very moment when Jesus ascended back to heaven: "Why are you standing there looking up at the sky? This Jesus, who was taken from you into heaven, *will come back*" (Acts 1:11). And this is why, a few days later, Peter is soon saying to the religious leaders in Jerusalem:

> *"God will send Jesus. ... He must remain in heaven until the time comes for all things to be made new."*
>
> ACTS 3:20–21

In other words, *Jesus will return*; his followers can look forward to what is known as his 'second coming'*; at that time, they will be reunited with him. What a great reunion!

Jesus had hinted at this awesome truth during his ministry. Presumably, however, his words made little sense at the time – after all, if his followers could not yet understand his death and resurrection, how much less any talk of a return *after that*! But now, the Spirit would have brought back to their minds key parts of his teaching, for example:

- his parables about a master returning to find his servants not working (e.g. Matthew 24 – 25, Mark 13:34–37, Luke 21:25–38);
- his warnings to be alert for the appearing of "the Son of Man ... coming in the clouds with great power" (Mark 13:26) and not to be 'ashamed' of him on that day (Mark 8:38);
- his puzzling words in the upper room: "I will come back to you" (John 14:18, 28).

Although these words may well have had other layers of meaning, the conviction grew that they also referred to Jesus' return at the final end of human history – his 'second coming'.

But when would that be? They simply did not know. For Jesus himself had made it abundantly clear:

> *"No one knows ... when that day or hour will come – neither the angels in heaven, nor the Son; only the Father knows. ... Be on guard, then, because you do not know when the master of the house is coming."*
>
> MARK 13:32, 35

Although it was sorely tempting to speculate, trying to discern the 'signs of the times', the apostles had to encourage Jesus' followers to live in the keen expectation that Jesus' return might occur *at any moment* and without prior warning – 'as a thief comes at night' (1 Thessalonians 4:15 – 5:11). At some point, 'the Lord Jesus would appear from heaven with his mighty angels' (2 Thessalonians 1:7ff); believers were to '*wait* for God's Son to come from heaven' (1 Thessalonians 1:10). And they were not to worry if believers had already died; those believers would 'rise to life first', so that all the faithful, past and present, could enjoy the Lord's presence together (1 Thessalonians 4:16–17). With this hope so strong in their hearts, it is not surprising that the earliest prayer to have survived from New Testament believers (preserved in Aramaic*) is "*Marana tha* – Our Lord, come!" (1 Corinthians 16:22).

Even so, the apostles also prepared people for the possibility of a delay:

> *Some people ... will mock you and will ask, "He promised to come, didn't he? Where is he?" ...*
>
> *But ... there is no difference in the LORD's sight between one day and a thousand years. ... The LORD is not slow to do what he has promised, as some think. Instead, he is patient with you, because he does not want anyone to be destroyed, but wants all to turn away from their sins.*
>
> 2 PETER 3:3–4, 8–9

The reason why Jesus has not yet returned, according to Peter here, is that God wants as many people as possible to respond to his Good News. As Jesus had expressly stated, the Good News had first to be "preached to all peoples" (Mark 13:10). So, even though people may find this future event quite difficult to imagine, we should not mock this idea of Jesus' second coming. The Greek word (*parousia*), which is often translated as 'second coming' actually means something more like the 'personal, royal presence' of a king. Thus, although he did not know the precise means, Peter was convinced that one day, believers would be in the *personal, royal presence* of God's appointed king, Jesus. We will be brought 'faultless and joyful before his glorious presence' (Jude 24).

Elsewhere, the apostles use other images to describe that incredible day when believers will meet with Jesus face to face: we will be 'with Christ' (Philippians 1:23), 'share God's eternal glory' (1 Peter 5:10) and *ourselves* 'appear before Christ' (2 Corinthians 5:10). Jesus prayed that his followers might be with him where he is, so that they could see his 'glory' (John 17:24). And, on that day, his prayer will be answered. We will see the king!

> *Peter was convinced that one day, believers would be in the personal, royal presence of God's appointed king, Jesus.*

Resurrection for the believer

Finally (as these last few verses have indicated), the resurrection of Jesus teaches us something very important about ourselves. Our death is not our end. There is life beyond the grave. Into the darkness of the ancient world, with its despair about the possibility of life beyond death, came the light of Jesus' resurrection. Jesus' coming, the apostles teach, has now 'set free those who were slaves all their lives because of their fear of death' (Hebrews 2:15). In Jesus' resurrection,

> God has ended the power of death and through the gospel
> has revealed immortal life.
>
> 2 TIMOTHY 1:10

For those who are fearful of death, Jesus' resurrection is indeed Good News. However, for those who think (or even wish) that death *is* the end, the resurrection is bad news. Thus many people, neither believing in God nor in life after death, act in a way that Paul condemns: "Let us eat and drink," they say, "for tomorrow we will die" (1 Corinthians 15:32). It is a sad way to live — exploiting physical pleasures now, minimising pain, and never finding any true meaning; life is lived under a black cloud and on a road that, so it appears, leads nowhere. Yet, in the light of the resurrection, it is also a foolish and dangerous way to live, becauseJesus' resurrection means not only that death is not the end. It also means that we will all meet Jesus after we die.

Box 12b – The apostles' teaching: judgement after death

Everyone must die once, and after that be judged by God.

HEBREWS 9:27

All of us must appear before Christ, to be judged by him.

2 CORINTHIANS 5:10

It is a terrifying thing to fall into the hands of the living God!

HEBREWS 10:31

God has fixed a day in which he will judge the whole world with justice by means of a man he has chosen. He has given proof of this to everyone by raising that man from death!

ACTS 17:31

For other related passages, see Matthew 7:23; 25:1–46; John 3:18; 5:27–30; Romans 2:9; 3:19.

For believers in Jesus, however, the resurrection is the best news in the world. It is a pledge and foretaste of eternal life (or life in the 'age to come': Mark 10:20). Jesus said,

> "I am the resurrection and the life. Those who believe in me will live, even though they die."

JOHN 11:25

> If we are truly followers of Jesus, this is now our destiny – to be with him for ever!

He is acknowledging that believers will still die physically, but promising that they will continue to be alive; a few chapters later, he expressly promises that he is going to 'prepare a place' for his followers so that they can be with him (John 14:2–3). 'And so,' writes Paul, 'we will always be with the Lord' (1 Thessalonians 4:17). If we are truly followers of Jesus, this is now our destiny – to be with him for ever!

It's worth reading Paul's great chapter about the believer's resurrection body (1 Corinthians 15; extracts given in Box 12a).

Because of Jesus' physical resurrection from the dead, believers can look forward to a similar resurrection. Our bodies will not be discarded, but we will be given new 'spiritual bodies' – real bodies, but animated by God's Spirit and able to live in God's new creation.

Living in hope

These three strands make up the confident hope of New Testament Christianity. Because of Jesus' resurrection, we know God has a future – not only for Jesus himself, but also for those who believe in him, and indeed for this world. Jesus will be seen again, we will be given new resurrection bodies, and God will bring this all together in an act of new creation.

We are therefore to be people marked by hope. In Box 12a we see how the lives of the first Christians were marked by this quality – what Peter calls this 'living hope', which 'cannot decay or spoil'. So he tells Jesus' followers always to be 'ready ... to explain the hope you have in you' (1 Peter 3:15). Similarly, John notes how this hope should cause us to live holy lives (1 John 3:3), whilst Paul elsewhere encourages us not to grieve in the face of death: we are not to be 'sad as are those who have no hope' (1 Thessalonians 4:13).

> God wants us to live lives marked, not by insecurity and uncertainty, but by confident hope.

This should encourage us in our following of Jesus. For there is nothing like a strong tonic of biblical hope to keep us following him – motivated for the journey and inspired by its glorious ending. If tempted to give up, we should lift up our eyes and consider again this great hope which God has given us – found only in Jesus. God wants us to live lives marked, not by insecurity and uncertainty, but by confident hope.

Indeed, the Christian life should be seen as a life lived *in the interval between two great fixed points* – the victory of Jesus in his death and resurrection (in the past), and the ultimate victory of Jesus (in the future) when we too will be raised. So we can live our lives, as it were, like a trapeze artist walking between these two fixed poles – knowing too that underneath us, like a safety net, are the 'eternal arms' of God (Deuteronomy 33:27).

So, although Jesus warned us that we would be made to suffer in this world (John 16:33), he also assured us that he can give us his peace, which he does not give "as the world does" (John 14:27). Moreover, we will have many life decisions to make, but we can bring these to Jesus too. For if Jesus can take care of the future of the whole world, he can surely take care of our individual futures. We may not know our own future in any detail, but we do now know *him who holds that future* in his hand.

The question is: will we trust him as we go into this unknown future? Or will we doubt his power, his love or his wisdom? Will we pray for his world and work hard for its renewal and for Jesus' kingdom to come – even on days when evil seems rampant? And will we prepare ourselves for his return – even when there seems so long a delay?

> *Let us run the race. ... Let us keep our eyes fixed on Jesus, on whom our faith depends from beginning to end (Hebrews 12:1–2).*

To follow Jesus is indeed to set out on a journey, which often can be more difficult than we ever imagined at first. Yet the Bible teaches us that Jesus himself has already run this race: 'Let us run the race. ... Let us keep our eyes fixed on Jesus, on whom our faith depends from beginning to end' (Hebrews 12:1–2). In other words, Jesus has blazed a trail ahead of us. And now (as the one who brings our faith to completion) he is standing at the finishing line, beckoning us forwards.

The twelfth building-block in the Christian life, then, is to keep our eyes fixed on Jesus and to reach out our hand, placing it in his, for he is our trustworthy companion. We are to *trust him for the future*, knowing that he has conquered all that is evil and that our future is safe in his hands.

Building-block 12

Trust Him for the Future – His Victory is Assured!

EPILOGUE

You will be well aware by now that I want you to follow Jesus. Also that I think the New Testament is not just a brilliant guide, but a vital one, if we are ever going to follow him truly. Jesus *did* give clear guidance to his apostles; and their own guidance, found in the pages of the New Testament, is a reliable guide for us today.

This book has given you a brief introduction to the apostles' writings in the New Testament, but I hope you will now be motivated to discover its treasures for yourself. For the reasons given in the Introduction (not least that many people in the world still may not have access to their own copy of the Bible), I have tried to draw out the meaning of the whole New Testament through the lens of just *two* of its 257 chapters (Luke 24 and Acts 2). I hope this has given you a sense of how powerful this small, ancient book is. But now, if you have the opportunity, how about reading more of it for yourself? Why not look up some of the references already mentioned? Or how about sitting down to read one of the gospels or one of Paul's letters? These will help you so much in your walk with Jesus. *There is nothing like reading the Bible for ourselves.*

Dividing the material into twelve chapters may also have been useful for various reasons — not least because it provides a framework that could easily be committed to memory. Moreover, it is not just that the first six chapters (in part 1) come directly from the teaching of Jesus, and the second six (in part 2) from the teaching and example of the apostles, his first followers. You will find that these two halves match each other in even closer ways (see the diagram overleaf).

In other words, we find that in part 2 we have worked through essentially the same six themes, but in the reverse order. For example, in chapter 1 we focused on the resurrection but concentrated on what it means to meet with the Risen Jesus today; in chapter 12 on what the resurrection means instead for the world and for our future. Again, in chapter 2 we focused on the cross as the place where our sins were forgiven; but in chapter 11 on it as the place where evil was conquered, so that we too must now fight sin and evil. And so on. You may find it helpful to go back through the material and note this pattern.

Bear Witness to His Reign	**6**	RELATING TO OTHERS	**7**	Share with Jesus' People
Participate in His Meal	**5**	WORSHIP	**8**	Worship His Majesty
Feed on His Scriptures	**4**	SCRIPTURE	**9**	Follow His Teaching
Welcome His Spirit	**3**	SPIRIT	**10**	Live His Life
Receive His Forgiveness	**2**	CROSS	**11**	Resist His Enemy
Enjoy Jesus' Resurrection	**1**	RESURRECTION	**12**	Trust Him for the Future

At several points, we noted the way the different chapters balance each other in some intriguing ways. For example, the first three chapters highlight the Trinitarian truth of God *with* us, God *for* us, God *in* us. The second three chapters (4 to 6) have a focus *backwards* (to Scripture in studying), *upwards* (to God in worship) and *outwards* (to others in mission).

Meanwhile, chapters 3 to 5 outline consecutively three main emphases that regularly appear in Christian responses to the message of the cross and resurrection of Jesus: there can be those who give special focus to the Spirit, others to the Scriptures, others to the Sacrament of the Lord's Supper (often labelled, rightly or wrongly, as the 'charismatic', 'evangelical' and 'liturgical' emphases). Each of these is very important. Yet the fact that all three are followed in this book by the focus on *extending Jesus' kingdom* (in mission and service to others), helpfully puts these three emphases within a better context. For there is a danger that, on their own, they can be over-emphasised – that somehow they become *ends in themselves*. When, however, they are placed within the overriding concern of Jesus' mission to the world, they can resume their proper place.

We must remember that the church (that is, the company of all those seeking to be Jesus' followers) is, in the famous words of a former Archbishop of Canterbury (William Temple, 1881-1944) the only 'organisation in the world that exists for the benefits of its non-members'. The Risen Jesus calls us *inwards* to himself and *upwards* to God, but ultimately he also sends us *out* again in his name. So what we have been studying in this book is not only Jesus' recipe for the transformation of *your* small world, but his recipe for the transformation of the whole world – that is, *his* world.

If studying these pages helps you in your walk with Jesus, I will be glad, but remember too that Jesus himself is always walking outwards to others. The Jesus Way begins with Jesus and ends with Jesus. Yet, along the way, we are to bring others onto the road, and play our part in implementing his kingdom within his world.

We Are to Follow Jesus
– *His* Way!

APPENDICES

APPENDIX A

Jesus of Nazareth: What Makes Him Unique?

Some readers may still be uncertain about whether it is worth setting out on the Jesus Way. Others may want to encourage their friends to follow Jesus but don't know what they can say that might encourage them to take this matter seriously. Whichever group you find yourself in, here are five things about Jesus which, taken all together, mark him out to be quite unique.

1. No one has ever *taught* as this man

Those who heard him teach could not believe their ears. Unlike their normal religious teachers, Jesus 'taught with authority'. "Where did he get such wisdom?" they asked.

So, despite his use of simple illustrations, his teaching has proved enduringly profound: one collection of his sayings (the Sermon on the Mount) is probably the most famous sermon of all time. One of his followers, when some in the crowd were finding Jesus' teaching too challenging, explained why he could not give up following Jesus: "You have *the words that give eternal life.*"

Jesus' teaching was stunningly powerful, exact and liberating – it brought life. "I am telling you the truth ..." It was true and authoritative because it stemmed from his direct and personal knowledge of God. Thus, where others spoke *about* God, this man spoke as though *from* God. In other words, Jesus not only knew *what* he was talking about; more importantly, he knew *who* he was talking about.

2. No one has ever *lived* as this man

Our closest friends know our own weaknesses all too well. Not so with Jesus. Looking back on his life, his closest followers concluded that he had 'committed no sin', and that in him there had been no 'sin' or 'darkness' whatsoever (see 1 Peter 2:22; 1 John 1:5; 3:3–6).

Instead he claimed to be the 'light of the world' and challenged his accusers directly: "Which one of you can prove that I am guilty of sin?" (John 8:12, 46). There was no answer. For this reason, none of the charges brought against him, when he was later on trial, focused on any of his supposed moral failings, but focused instead on religious and political disagreements.

What people sensed when they were with Jesus was the perfect combination of attributes that in others are often out of balance: authority, power, strength of character, even gutsy determination, but all these shot through with humility, gentleness, compassion and grace; holiness but transforming love; a 'man of sorrows and familiar with suffering' but, simultaneously, a man full of life and the deepest joy (see Isaiah 53:6 NIV; Luke 10:21).

3. No one has ever *died* as this man

Other religious leaders associated with worldwide faiths have died in their beds. Not so Jesus.

His was a life marked by suffering: charged with being an illegitimate child, he was frequently misunderstood and often on the move. Eventually, in his mid-30s, he was betrayed into enemy hands by one of his friends, given a mockery of a trial, and then sentenced to what has been described as the cruellest death imaginable—crucifixion on a Roman cross. After floggings and beatings (which often were quite enough in themselves to bring about a victim's death), he was strung up on a piece of wood outside Jerusalem's walls, with nails driven through his wrists and legs — left there to suffocate, unable to breathe, and to die some three hours later.

Yes, there were many others in the ancient world (all of them slaves or political rebels) whom the Romans put through this hideous punishment, but none of them *actively chose this path* for themselves. Jesus did: he went up to Jerusalem, clearly predicting his death and actively encouraging others too to 'take up their cross'. And he asked his followers to remember him afterwards by focusing not on his life but on his death — his 'broken body' and 'shed blood'.

So Jesus' death, though excruciating, was chosen and intentional.His purpose, he said, was "to give his life to redeem many people"; his blood was to be shed "for the forgiveness of sins".

There is much more we could say, but clearly this was a death with a difference, involving desperate pain but for some deep purpose (see above chapter 2).

4. No one has ever *claimed as much* as this man

For all his evident humility, Jesus' teaching constantly forced his hearers to ask: who exactly *is* this teacher? Who does he think he is?

Within their shared history, they had great heroes, ancient institutions and holy writings; but now Jesus claimed to be 'greater than Solomon', 'greater than the Temple', the one in whom their Scriptures (the Old Testament) were coming true 'in their own hearing' (see Matthew 12:42; 12:6; Luke 4:21).

Moses, they believed, had brought down God's revealed Law from Mount Sinai, but now Jesus sat on a mountain and said: "You have heard that people were told in the past, but now *I* tell you..." People were longing for God to become king, but now Jesus in proclaiming the arrival of God's kingdom made it clear that he was not only the doorkeeper (who decided who would enter the kingdom) but none other than the *king himself* (see Matthew 5:21–22; Luke 13:27).

Carefully choosing his words, Jesus claimed to be Israel's anointed king (Messiah), the exalted figure known as the 'Son of Man' who would judge the world, and the 'Son' whom the 'Father' (God) was fully trusting. Indeed he dared to use God's name ("I AM" – revealed in Exodus 3:14) and apply it in various ways directly to himself (see Matthew 25:31; Mark 8:29–31; Luke 10:22; John 6:37; 8:12, 58).

Hearing such claims, some ever since have thought him mad or bad, but others, sensing his sanity and sincerity, have concluded that he knew exactly who he was, and also that his claims – however unparalleled in human history – are true.

5. No one has ever *been worshipped* as this man

Set against his Jewish culture (in which people were trained to proclaim regularly that there was only one God who alone was to be worshipped), it is remarkable that Jesus' first followers clearly felt compelled to worship him. This took place both during his lifetime and immediately afterwards – and indeed has continued to the present day.

After one of his miracles, his followers 'worshipped him', and later a follower called Thomas, himself prone to doubt and questioning, was moved to call Jesus "My Lord and my God!" Thereafter, his followers in their writings always bracketed Jesus together with God (calling him the 'Lord', the 'Son of God' etc.) and encouraged others to worship and 'glorify' him. No other worldwide faith worships its human founder in this blatant way (see Matthew 14:33; John 20:28; Galatians1:1; Philippians 2:11, etc.).

* * *

These five factors concerning Jesus suggest that he is indeed unique – in a class of his own. They also explain why no one has ever been *followed* as this man. Throughout history and to this present day, millions of people have been followers of Jesus. To follow Jesus, then, is not to set out on one's own, but rather to do so in the company of countless others.

APPENDIX B

The Resurrection of Jesus: Can We Be Sure?

The bodily resurrection of Jesus from death stands at the very centre of the Christian faith. So it's worth looking briefly at some of the arguments which point towards this being a real historical event.

Given that we are dealing here with a one-off event which took place nearly 2,000 years ago, we cannot ultimately provide incontrovertible 'proof' – historical events in that sense are not 'provable'. Yet there have been serious-minded people (including many people initially prone to scepticism) who have come to the conclusion that this is one of the best-attested facts of ancient history. We would do well to follow their reasoning.

What, then, are the arguments used against the truth of the resurrection and how might we answer them?

Contrary to history and science?

Many objections to the resurrection include catchphrases such as these: "Dead men don't rise!" "Miracles don't happen nowadays – and never did!" Indeed, many of the most thoughtful objections to the resurrection have this form, effectively pointing out that the resurrection, if it occurred, would have been a unique event in the world's history. Such a one-off miracle, we are then told, appears to break the rules of both history and science.

However, that does not necessarily mean that it did not happen. For history and science can only *observe* what happens – they cannot *dictate* what happens. On the contrary, if the resurrection *did* occur, then it means we have to rethink what we mean by 'science' and 'history'.

So, if anyone affirms the truth of the resurrection, this does not mean they are giving up on science. Instead, they are being open to the possibility that God can work in his world – both in scientifically observable ways, and also occasionally in ways that break the pattern (often called 'miracles'). Moreover, what if, in the resurrection, God was doing something that he will be doing again at some point in the future? In that case, the resurrection would not always remain unique. Jesus' resurrection might instead just be a *foretaste* of what God will do when he raises others at the end of time. At that point, therefore, there would be many 'scientific' parallels to this event — it's just that we have not seen them yet!

Again, if anyone affirms the truth of the resurrection, this does not mean they are giving up on history. Instead, they are simply being open to where the evidence has been leading them. Often, historians have to work back from known historical facts to posit an earlier event which alone explains those later consequences. This is what we see with Jesus' resurrection: there are some surprising things that happen subsequently that demand an adequate explanation. And the best explanation — historically — may be the resurrection of Jesus. Only *this* adequately explains *that*.

Box B contains a list of these 'surprising things' which took place after the resurrection and which demand some kind of historical explanation.

Box B — Questions requiring a historian's answer

- What changed Jesus' fearful and frightened followers into brave and courageous witnesses, ready to die for him?

- Why did they start referring to him as 'Lord' and the 'Son of God' when *as Jews* they believed that their God, 'the Lord', was the 'the Lord alone' (Deuteronomy 6:4)?

- Why did the first Christians change their day of worship from the Jewish Sabbath (on Saturday) to Sunday? And why did they worship God by sharing in a meal that focused in a macabre way on the cruel death of their founder?

- What explains the rapid spread of this Jewish messianic sect across the Greco-Roman world in the first century? And, if the task of the 'Messiah' was to rid Israel of its pagan occupiers and to establish a reign of peace, why did the first Christians proclaim Jesus as the Messiah? Apparently Jesus had achieved neither of these things; instead, his death on a Roman cross strongly suggested that he was a *failed* Messiah. So what caused Christians to make this absurd claim in the face of this evidence to the contrary?

- Why does the New Testament use a word for 'resurrection' (*anastasis*) which means literally 'making to stand upright'? This word never referred to some merely 'spiritual' event but to the stark event when a dead body was raised in a physical sense. One group within Judaism (the Pharisees) firmly believed that this would happen to all God's people at the end of time; other Jews doubted this. Meanwhile, those in the pagan world knew for a fact that it did not happen — "dead men don't rise!" Why did the first Christians use this word — a word inviting ridicule and scorn — when it would have been so much easier to speak of some more 'mystical' experience?

- Why does the New Testament make this startling concept of resurrection (both of Jesus and then of believers) so central in its thinking — especially when compared with the Old Testament, which mentions resurrection so rarely?

All of these are intriguing historical facts from the first century *which make very little sense if the resurrection did not happen*. Some of them may seem rather technical, yet they are important questions for historians nonetheless. Together, they build up a cumulative case which *points back* to the resurrection of Jesus as a real event that occurred in real history. Each of them is a manifest fact from within ancient history — no one can seriously deny that these things happened. The question is: why? Go through the list and ask yourself whether any one of these would have happened if Jesus was known to be dead and buried.

So Jesus' resurrection, though a unique event, cannot be ruled out in advance as somehow non-scientific or non-historical. Instead, it requires careful investigation.

Just a 'spiritual' resurrection?

Moving on, other objections to the resurrection begin to focus instead on raising questions about the early Christians' claims. For example, what if Jesus' followers came to believe in his resurrection *by mistake*? Perhaps they just got in a muddle? Perhaps Jesus' corpse was still there, but they mistakenly went to the wrong tomb? Yet, even if there was some initial confusion after dawn that Sunday morning the correct tomb was only a few yards away. And, when you look at Box B again, it's reasonably clear that Jesus' followers were basing their actions on something more than just muddled thinking.

At this point, people often suggest that Jesus' followers were only talking of a 'spiritual' resurrection, not a brute physical one. If so, Jesus' followers did not make a *mistake* as such (believing Jesus was physically raised, when in fact he was still in the tomb). Instead, what they did (on this argument) was sincerely to conclude that somehow he was alive again, but only in some kind of spiritual sense.

This novel idea, however, when examined, turns out to be very vague. Jesus' followers are attributed with notions such as these: that 'Jesus was too good to die'; or that they could 'still sense his influence' upon their lives. These are nice thoughts, but they fail entirely to explain three things:

- why people then started calling Jesus 'Messiah' and 'Lord' (when, being dead, he clearly was *not!*);
- why people were willing to die for this still-dead Jesus;
- why people started talking (as Jesus' followers clearly did, immediately) about *anastasis* – a Greek word which (literally) means Jesus 'stood up' vertically, no longer being a corpse lying horizontally in a grave.

Jesus' followers repeatedly made these outrageous claims, and stuck to them in the face of strong opposition. Why?

We conclude, then, that Jesus' first followers would never have conceded that Jesus' corpse was still lying in the tomb. Nor could they have started out merely with a notion that Jesus was 'alive' in some vague spiritual sense, and then only later become convinced that the tomb had been empty. No, as far as they were concerned, the tomb was empty from the outset. All their talk about a resurrection (a physical 'raising up' of a body from the dead) would never have even started – never 'got off the ground' – if Jesus' corpse was still in the tomb.

Dealing with the empty tomb

The question becomes: how come the tomb was empty? We need an explanation. And only three options are possible:

- Jesus had not truly died; so, once he revived, he walked out of the tomb on his own.
- Jesus' corpse was stolen.
- Jesus was raised from the dead by an act of God.

Option A is absurd

Roman soldiers would have ensured any crucified 'criminal' was truly dead before allowing his body to be removed. This is precisely why they pierced Jesus' side before bringing him down from the cross (John 19). What flowed out from the spear wound was serum and water – a sure sign (not understood at the time) that death had already occurred. Jesus was clearly dead.

Yet, even supposing that he was not quite dead, we may reasonably ask how likely it is that, after all his suffering (and then 36 hours left on a cold, damp slab — without any medical attention), Jesus would somehow revive, push away the entrance stone and convince people that he had conquered death? To believe this almost takes more faith than to believe in the resurrection!

Option B is very unlikely

Who would want to steal the body? The Roman and Jewish authorities both had a keen interest in suppressing any further interest in Jesus. So they would hardly have stolen the body. And, if they had, then surely they would have produced it as soon as anyone started making these strange claims that Jesus had been raised from the dead: "Oh no, he hasn't – here's the corpse!"

But could Jesus' corpse have been stolen, not by his enemies, but by his *friends*? This was the first explanation given by the guards and it remained a popular theory amongst Jerusalem's populace right up until the time of Matthew's gospel (see Matthew 28:15).

Yet, although it seemed plausible to ancient critics, it remains most unlikely. For Jesus' followers were in no mood for any heroics involving such risky corpse-snatching. Such activity was a criminal offence and would have brought them immediately to the authorities' attention. That was the last thing they wanted. Ten of Jesus' twelve disciples had been so frightened at the time of Jesus' arrest that they had fled out of the city and over the Mount of Olives – fearing they too would be arrested. No, Jesus' followers were very much 'on the back foot'; they were depressed and fearful for their lives.

So they were not going to be stealing Jesus' corpse. And, anyway, what was the point? The grave, which a wealthy follower named Joseph of Arimathea had provided for Jesus, was far better than anything his poor friends from Galilee could have mustered up at short notice. What Jesus' body needed was not a relocating but rather a more thorough anointing – precisely what the women then planned to accomplish on the Sunday morning.

This all then explains why, when Jesus' friends first heard the news that his body had disappeared, they were so fearful and distraught. This was not good news at all in their eyes – it was a complete disaster! For they would now be accused of stealing it, and that is precisely what they did not want.

So it seems reasonably clear that the disciples did not steal it. Moreover, if they *had* stolen it, we would then have to believe that they gave up the rest of their lives proclaiming a message about Jesus – at great personal risk to themselves – *which they knew to be a complete lie*. Once again, this is psychologically implausible. And surely, once persecution came their way, one of their number would have snapped under pressure and leaked the truth. But they never did.

Option C

We are left with the answer that Jesus' followers gave from the outset, namely that *Jesus had been raised from the dead by God himself*. As we saw, they themselves could not believe it at first. So they knew full well that it would sound absurd to others, but there was no other explanation. We too need to ask ourselves: is there an alternative explanation which makes any sense?

Jesus was seen again

Finally, we must not forget that Jesus' followers made this claim for one other vitally important reason: because Jesus himself had met them! On that first Easter Sunday, according to Luke 24, Jesus 'appeared to

Simon', to the Emmaus disciples, and also to those gathered in the upper room. Here's how Paul put it, some 20 years later:

> I passed on to you what I received, which is of the greatest importance: that Christ died for our sins, as written in the Scriptures; that he was buried and that he was raised to life three days later, as written in the Scriptures; that he appeared to Peter and then to all twelve apostles. Then he appeared to more than five hundred of his followers at once, most of whom are still alive, although some have died. Then he appeared to James, and afterwards to all the apostles.
> The truth is that Christ has been raised from death ...
>
> 1 CORINTHIANS 15:3–7, 20

In other words, there are people still living, says Paul, who can vouch for what we are saying. The resurrection is part of the essential message of Christianity ('of the greatest importance'); there is no Good News without it. And its truth is assured by the simple, but amazing, fact that the Risen Jesus was seen on a number of occasions. These were not hallucinations, nor just a delayed reaction within their grief process. No, *these were real encounters with Jesus*. Initially, writes Luke, Jesus' followers thought that they were 'seeing a ghost', but then Jesus proceeded to eat some boiled fish before their very eyes! This was their master, Jesus, now back from the dead.

Luke wants any followers of Jesus – then or now – to be convinced about Jesus' resurrection: a real death was followed by an empty tomb, and then by real encounters with the Risen Jesus. This was not something just in the minds of Jesus' followers (perhaps invented to make them feel better). No, it was something that happened *in the real life-story of Jesus himself*.

And the consequence is: this same Jesus is alive today. As Paul puts it: 'Christ has been raised from death and will never die again – death will no longer rule over him' (Romans 6:9). The resurrection of Jesus thus turns out to be not just a remarkable event within ancient history. Far more than that, it is the event which brings Jesus from the past into the present – able to meet with people today and to transform their lives.

APPENDIX C

Baptism for Jesus' Followers: Why is it Important?

At the very end of his ministry on earth, Jesus gave his first followers a clear instruction: "Go, then, to all peoples everywhere and make them my disciples: baptize them in the name of the Father, the Son, and the Holy Spirit, and teach them to obey everything I have commanded you" (Matthew 28:19–20).

Jesus evidently wants his followers to be well taught but also to be 'baptised'. In *The Jesus Way* we have focused on the first of these, aiming to give a good summary of Jesus' teaching, but we also need to explain here the meaning of 'baptism': what is it and why is it important? Why did Jesus want his followers to go through this ritual?

Joining God's people

The word 'baptism' comes from the ordinary Greek word for 'washing'. However it came to be used in a restricted sense to apply to a washing done for specifically religious reasons. By the time of Jesus, various such baptisms had developed within Jewish practice, one of which was designed for non-Jews who wished now to belong to God's people (the nation of Israel). So baptism was, first, all about joining God's people.

This was why John the Baptist's call to his fellow Israelites was so controversial: he was effectively saying that, despite belonging by birth to God's historic people, they needed now to *re*join God's people – to start all over again. It was no good claiming that they had Abraham as their 'father'; each person now had to make their own humble entrance into God's new people (see Luke 3).

So the baptism Jesus commands is an outward sign that we belong to his people – it's like a badge of membership. All Jesus' followers have gone through this same 'rite of initiation'. So, when we ourselves are baptised, we join this group of people who have all been through the same experience. Jesus himself was baptised (by John in the River Jordan – see e.g. Matthew 3:13–17) and this has been true for all his followers ever since. In the books of Acts, there are numerous episodes in which we see people responding to the message of Jesus and promptly being baptised (see e.g. Acts 2:41; 8:38; 9:18; 10:48). It is the clear signal that individuals have joined Jesus' new people.

Repenting and receiving the Spirit

When joining any new group or society, we have to make certain commitments, or assent to various beliefs. It's no different here. Baptism can never be just an empty formula, in which we 'go through the motions', but is meant to be an outward sign of our inner choices and commitments. The very first sermon by the apostle Peter closes with these important words which make this point:

> "Each one of you must turn away from your sins and be baptized in the name of Jesus Christ, so that your sins will be forgiven; and you will receive God's gift, the Holy Spirit. For God's promise was made to you and your children, and to all who are far away – all whom the Lord our God calls to himself."
>
> ACTS 2:38–39

Peter makes it crystal clear that only those who have repented from their sins should consider getting baptised. The key point in following Jesus is recognising that he is the one who offers us 'forgiveness of sins' (see above, chapter 2). This means we cannot choose to follow him without recognising this: in other words, we have to recognise our sinfulness, repent, and seek his forgiveness. Baptism, then, is the public sign of our more private decision – namely that we have repented of our sins and are now turning from all that is evil. We are turning from darkness to the light of Christ.

As we have seen (above, chapter 3), those who come to Christ in this way not only receive God's forgiveness but also receive his Holy Spirit. This second great truth is then reflected in Peter's words: those who repent "receive God's gift, the Holy Spirit". Baptism then becomes a sign of this too: that we are not just *repentant* people who have been *forgiven*, but also *empty* people who have now been *filled*. Of course, the very act of baptism *cannot actually bring about* this spiritual reality, any more than it can bring us automatically the forgiveness of our sins (these invisible realities only come about through exercising repentant faith in Jesus). Yet baptism remains the outward and visible sign of these great realities, which have truly come about in the life of every one of Jesus' followers.

Baptism therefore has within it a pattern of death and resurrection: dying to sin and then coming to a new Spirit-filled life in Christ. That's why Paul in Romans 6 can speak of us being 'buried with Christ' in our baptism and rising to 'new life'. We can also see how baptism draws together the three great truths we looked at in the first three chapters of *The Jesus Way*: believing in Jesus as the Risen Lord, repenting from our sins (for which he died on the cross) and receiving his Holy Spirit.

So, if you have taken those three steps but have not yet been baptised, it's important now to go forward to baptism as soon as possible. This will involve talking with a leader in your local church and then preparing appropriately for this important event in your new Christian life.

A baptism can be a great time of celebration! It's a way of publicly showing our new commitment to Jesus' way and receiving God's assurance that we are now his. And, once we are baptised, we find we are part of God's new people and can then enjoy coming to the family's 'meal' (chapter 5). Throughout the past 2,000 years, the meal of the 'Lord's Supper' has always been preserved as a meal designed only for those who have first been baptised. So here's another reason why baptism is important: if we wish to participate in the 'breaking of bread' with other believers, we must first be baptised. No baptism, no meal.

Practical details

Sometimes people can be anxious about what precisely their baptism will involve in practice. Of course, this will vary from place to place, as different churches follow different customs. In terms of its essential ingredients, however, a baptism always involves two things:

- **Some water.** Sometimes people go down into some water, totally submerged, and then come up again; sometimes they are just sprinkled with water. Although different churches have adopted different positions on this point, arguably both practices have biblical support (see e.g. Acts 8:38–39 and 1 Peter 1:2 NIV). In fact, the standard practice of the early church seems to have been a combination of the two: baptismal candidates would stand in some running water (perhaps up to their knees) but then have this water scooped up and poured over their heads.

- **A prayer in the name of the Trinity.** Although the New Testament often talks about people being baptised 'in the name of Jesus', Jesus' authoritative words in Matthew 28 (quoted just above) have always been taken as giving the full formula which should be used: we are to be baptised "in the name of the Father, the Son, and the Holy Spirit".

Finally, there is the complex issue that some people will have been baptised as an infant, when their parents had them 'christened'. We cannot go into detail here as to why this practice of infant baptism arose so early in the church's life (it had to do with emphasising how children are indeed to be seen as belonging in God's people). Yet, if this is true for you and you discover you have indeed already been baptised, then the best practice is to ask if you can now *publicly renew your baptismal vows as a believing adult*. This avoids the need for going through a 'repeat baptism' (as if the first one was ineffective), but gives you the opportunity now publicly to declare your faith in Jesus. In this way, your baptism as a child comes, as it were, to fulfilment — as you now express the repentant faith in Jesus that was presumed (and indeed prayed for!) at the start of your life.

GLOSSARY

Abba

This is the word for 'father' in Aramaic (Jesus' mother-tongue, still spoken in parts of modern Syria). The Gospels (themselves written in Greek) record only four or five Aramaic words, but this word, used by Jesus in praying to God (e.g. Mark 14:36), was treasured by the disciples – not least because it was a colloquial word used between a child and his father (like 'my Dad!'). Paul then encourages Christians, as God's adopted children, to address God in these intimate terms (Rom. 8:15; Gal. 4:6).

Agape love

This is one of four Greek words for 'love'. As opposed to mere 'friendship' or 'sexual love', this *agape* love is a selfless, outgoing concern for others. The apostles saw this as having been revealed supremely in Jesus and urged believers to express this love towards each other (see especially Paul's so-called 'hymn to love' in 1 Cor. 13; see also John 13:34; 1 John 4:7-21).

Amen

This is a Hebrew word meaning 'truly' or 'so be it'. It is a way of affirming and giving assent to what has been prayed – meaning "it's true!" or "Yes, Lord!"

Apostle

An 'apostle' is, literally, 'one who is sent out' (with a mission or task). In biblical thought the 'persons sent' (or commissioned as messengers) were to be received by others with the deference due to the 'person who sent them'. Jesus expected this for his own 'apostles' (Matt. 10:37), so we too should receive his apostles' teaching in the same way as we would receive Jesus himself. The evidence is strong that Jesus appointed an inner band of twelve apostles (reflecting the twelve tribes of Israel: see Matt. 19:28), but that Paul was effectively added to this number after his conversion (see 1 Cor. 9:1; 15:9). There will therefore be no new 'apostles' (in this strict, historical sense) – even though in every generation there will be many 'sent out' into the world in Jesus' name to do pioneering work for the kingdom.

Aramaic, *see Abba.*

Ascension of Jesus

Jesus' 'ascension', when Jesus finally returned to heaven, is the key event described by Luke between our two key chapters (Luke 24 and Acts 2). According to Acts 1:3, for a period of about 'forty days' the Risen Jesus had 'appeared to his followers in many ways that proved beyond doubt that he was alive', but this came to an end. For there came a day, when Jesus was on the Mount of Olives near Bethany, that 'he departed from them' and 'a cloud hid him from their sight' (see Luke 24:50-53; Acts 1:9-12). The New Testament sees this 'ascension' as the time when Jesus was exalted to the 'right hand' of God (Acts 2:33) and given the 'name that is greater than any other name' (Phil. 2:9); it was also when, as a sign of his finished work, he 'sat down', sharing the very throne of God (see Heb. 1:3; Eph. 1:20-23; Rev. 5:13).

Augustine of Hippo (AD 354-430)

Augustine was a pagan philosopher who was converted to Christian faith whilst reading the book of Romans in a garden in Milan in AD 387. His reflective autobiography (the *Confessions*) looks back on all that led up to this dramatic event. He is widely regarded as one of the greatest intellectuals of all time, and is honoured as one of the four great 'doctors' (or teachers) of the ancient church. The phrase 'faith seeking understanding' is often attributed to him, but is really a paraphrase of his words in his *Sermon* 43.7, 9: *'Crede, ut intelligas'* (Latin for 'believe in order that you may understand'). Meanwhile, the quote on p. 71 is from his *Confessions* 10.29.

Brothers and sisters

The Greek word *adelphoi* (meaning 'brothers and sisters') is used over 230 times in Acts and the Epistles to describe Christian believers – who have now been brought into God's family as equal members.

Canon

This word (derived from the Greek word for a 'rule', 'measuring-line' or 'benchmark') came to be used for the 'boundary-line' placed around Scripture, defining which books were to be included within the Bible (and thus 'canonical') and which books were to be 'ruled out'. This was a major issue in the 2nd century AD as the early church gathered together the various books of the New Testament and had to evaluate a wide variety of Christian literature, eventually categorising non-apostolic works as valuable but *'non-canonical'*.

Catholic

This comes from a Greek word which literally means 'throughout [or across] the world'. From the early 2nd century AD it was used as a key word to describe the amazing phenomenon of the Gospel of Jesus spreading across the world and thus creating a 'worldwide' or 'catholic' church.

Christology

This refers to the 'study of Christ's person', and describes all the debates which seek to answer the question, 'Who is Jesus?' Despite much debate, the New Testament writings show clear evidence of having a very strong or 'high' Christology, asserting that Jesus can be identified in some way with God himself – both in what he *does*, but also in who he essentially *is*. This was then well summarised in the **creed** (see ch. 9). See further R.J. Bauckham, *God Crucified*, Eerdmans, 1998.

Communion

This is one of the four terms commonly used to describe the meal instituted by Jesus at his Last Supper (see ch. 5). It picks up some words of Paul (1 Cor. 10:16), which speak of our *'participating'* in the body and blood of Christ (in older English 'communion' had this sense of 'participating with'). The other three terms are: *'Lord's Supper'*, which points to the truth that this is a meal, like the original Last Supper, which is hosted by Jesus (but now as the Risen Lord); *'Eucharist'*, which comes from the Greek word meaning 'thanksgiving'; and *'Mass'*, which comes from the Latin for 'dismissal' and echoes the words used at the end of many such communion services when people are 'dismissed' to their homes.

Over the years different theologies have become associated with each term, though the words themselves do not necessarily require those theologies. Each of the first three has clear biblical support, being used in Paul's discussion of this meal in 1 Corinthians 10-11. For evidence of how the first Christians conducted this meal, see Acts 2:42-46; 20:7; 1 Cor. 11:17-33; 16:2.

Church

This is the English word used to translate the New Testament word 'ekklesia'. Literally the word refers to those who have been 'called out'. It had been used in ancient Greece to describe the democratic civic 'assembly', but also in the Greek version of the Old Testament to describe God's 'chosen people'. The apostles see all believers as thus 'called out' or chosen by God through the gospel.

Confession

This describes when people 'confess' their sins to God, repenting of their wrongdoing. It literally means that they 'agree' with God and acknowledge that he is right and they are wrong (see e.g. Psa. 51:3-4). As seen in our opening chapters, it is a necessary part in any first response to the message about Jesus (the one who save from sins), but it should also form a continual part of a Christian's life (see 1 John 1:9). The apostles also encourage us on suitable occasions to 'confess our sins to one another' (see James 5:16); in some church traditions this has been formalised into making one's 'confession' before a 'priest', but, though this may be helpful, it is not something which the Bible requires.

Confirmation

This describes a special service or ritual which those churches who practise infant baptism normally encourage their members to pass through before they are allowed to receive the bread and wine at communion. It is designed to give people an opportunity as adults to confirm the promises made on their behalf at their baptism. It is also intended as a safeguard to ensure that those who come to communion are truly believers themselves. For those people who wish publicly to confirm their new-found faith in an even more dramatic way, most churches will also offer a special service for the 'renewal of baptism vows' (see Appendix C).

Covenant

This is a word frequently used in the Bible to describe the binding agreement and committed relationship which God establishes with his people (originally with Abraham and then with the people of Israel). It is well summarised in the divine promise: "I will be their God and they will be my people" (see e.g. Rev. 21:3). The closest parallel in ordinary life is the 'covenant' that binds together a husband and wife. The apostles teach that Jesus has inaugurated a 'new covenant' (as prophesied in Jeremiah 31) and that all believers in Jesus are thus members of God's 'covenant' people.

Creed

This is a short summary statement, articulating Christian faith ('credo' is Latin for 'I believe'). Several such 'creeds' were agreed and then recited regularly during the early church period (see ch. 9). Those used most frequently today are the 'Apostles' Creed' (a summary of the apostles' teaching dating to the late 2nd century) and the so-called 'Nicene' Creed (confusingly, composed at Constantinople in AD 381, though based on an earlier version promulgated at the Council of Nicaea in AD 325). The creeds do not have any authority above the Bible, but have an authority within the church – precisely because they have been shown over the centuries to be true to the Bible. Arguably, the creeds focus more on Jesus' *person* than on his *work* (i.e. his death on the cross and what that achieved for us), but this is because the debates about Jesus' p*erson and identity* were the most hotly disputed at that time. It was also because those compiling the creeds recognised that the achievement of the cross would be severely undermined if Jesus could not be identified in some way with God (see e.g. Rom 5:8; and above ch. 2).

Devil, the

There are clear hints concerning the Devil (also known as 'Satan' or the 'Evil One') in the Old Testament (see Gen. 3; Job 1); but the full revelation of his identity waits until the coming of Jesus. For references to Satan in the context of Jesus' ministry, see e.g. Mark 3:22-27; 8:33; Luke 4:1-13; 10:18; 22:31; 12:31; 14:30. For references in the apostles' teaching, see e.g. 1 John 3:8; 2 Cor. 11:14; 4:4; Eph. 2:1-3; 1 Thess. 3:5; 1 Tim. 4:1-2 and the accounts of exorcism in Acts 16:16-18, 19:13-20. Various pictures are used of the Devil: e.g. a snake (Gen. 3:1, 14-15; 2 Cor. 11:3), a devouring lion (1 Pet. 5:8-9) or a great dragon (Rev. 12:9). He is described as the 'father of lies' (John 8:44) and the 'accuser of the brethren' (Rev. 12:10).

Discipleship

Jesus' first followers are traditionally known as the 'disciples' – a word which simply means a 'learner', 'student' or 'someone in training'. So this is a good word too to describe Jesus' followers today. 'Discipleship' then becomes the word to describe the practical steps believers take to follow Jesus better day by day.

Docetism

This is the name for an early Christian movement which argued that Jesus, though truly God, only *appeared* to be human (from the Greek word 'to seem/appear'). This is denounced by the apostle John who insists that Jesus truly came 'in the flesh' (1 John 4:4; 2 John 7). This false teaching, of course, could only emerge once people had accepted the apostles' teaching about Jesus' *divinity* (as taught by John himself: see John 1:1-3, 14; 10:30; 20:28); so its existence confirms the high **Christology** that was present in the New Testament period.

Dualism, *see* Gnosticism

Easter

This word (derived from Old English) describes the season in the church's year which focuses on the resurrection of Jesus (celebrated on Easter Sunday). The Gospels writers clearly teach that Jesus' resurrection took place on the 'first day of the week' (i.e. a Sunday after the Jewish 'Sabbath'/Saturday). They are also clear that this was the first Sunday after the celebration of the **Passover** (which took place on the night of the spring-time full moon). From ancient times Christians have therefore celebrated the resurrection on the first

Sunday after the Passover full moon, but the date of this, of course, changes each year. There is continued debate as to whether the first Easter Sunday was April 9th, AD 30 or April 5th, AD 33.

Emmaus

This was a village to the north-west of Jerusalem. Four different locations have been suggested, with perhaps the most likely being the area of 'Motza' (now a suburb within modern Jerusalem): see my book, *In the Steps of Jesus* (LionHudson, 2007), pp. 204-5. If so, the distance covered by the two disciples (going to Emmaus and then back up to Jerusalem) would have been c. 7.5 miles (12 kilometres).

Eucharist, *see* Communion

Fellowship

This is the most common way of translating the New Testament references to '*koinonia*'. For an explanation of this term, see ch. 7.

Flesh

As discussed in chapter 11, the apostle Paul uses the word 'flesh' (*sarx* in Greek) in a specialist sense to speak of the sinful principle which is at work in human beings – in contrast to the 'spirit' (*pneuma* in Greek). Believers are to 'live according to the spirit', not 'according to the flesh': see Gal 5:16-17; Eph. 4:22-24, Rom. 6:1-11 and especially Rom. 8:13.

Gentiles

This is the way we translate into English the word used by Israel in the Old Testament for describing 'the nations' – those non-Jews outside Israel. Much of the New Testament is devoted to showing that through the gospel the time has now come for 'Gentiles' to enter God's people as Gentiles (that is, without their first needing to become Jews): see e.g. Gal. 2:15-21; Acts 15:1-36; Rom. 11:13-32; Eph. 2:11-14.

Gnosticism

Gnosticism was a 'heresy' (or 'false teaching'), which severely tested Jesus' followers in the generations after the New Testament. Its name comes from the Greek word for 'knowledge', because Gnostics developed elaborate systems of mystical paths, which those *in the know* could follow in pursuit of God. Influenced by Greek philosophy, Gnostic thought was strongly dualistic, setting up a strong contrast between created matter (seen as evil) and the spiritual realm; 'salvation' or 'enlightenment' was then a matter of escaping into that realm. In the 2nd and 3rd centuries AD Gnostic writers produced many rehashed versions of Jesus' teaching which, arguably, contain very littler reliable testimony to the authentic, historical Jesus. For early hints of Gnosticism within the New Testament, see e.g. 1 Tim. 6:20 or Col. 2:8, 16-23.

God-fearer

This was a word coined to describe the many Gentiles who were 'fringe' members of the Jewish synagogue – respecting and valuing Jewish ideals but not wishing formally to convert to Judaism (which for the men would have required circumcision). Almost certainly the author of Luke's Gospel had been a God-fearer, and many of the first converts to Christianity may well have been drawn from their number.

Homo-ousios

As noted in chapter 9, this strange Greek word (translated 'of one being with') appears in the **Nicene Creed**. At the time of the creed's composition some were arguing that Jesus was only '*like*' God (in Greek *homoios*), not *identical with* God (in Greek *homos*). In these circumstances the creed's compilers coined this new non-biblical word in order to safeguard that which *was* taught within the Bible – even if using different words – namely that Jesus can be identified with God (see John 1:14, 18; Heb. 1:3; Col. 1:15 etc). The incarnation of Jesus, being unique and unprecedented in human history, naturally required Christians to give new meanings to old words and sometimes (as here) to coin entirely new terminology.

Incarnation/incarnate

This word (derived from the Latin for 'in the flesh') picks up the teaching of John's Gospel, which speaks of Jesus as the Word of God who 'became flesh' (John 1:14). So the 'incarnation' is the unique event in which God entered our human world in the person of his Son, Jesus – sometimes referred to as 'God incarnate'.

Ingathering of the nations

There are numerous texts in the Old Testament which list Israel's hopes for what God would do in the future. One such hope was that the **Gentile** nations would acknowledge Israel's God and would be 'gathered in' – that is, coming up to Jerusalem and joining his people in worship (see e.g. Isa. 2:1-4; 19:16-25; 60:1-22; Psa. 87).

Jerusalem

This, the central city in Israel's history, was established as the nation's capital by King David, with its Temple being founded by his son, Solomon (in 970 BC). By the time of Jesus the city was under Roman occupation, but the Temple had been magnificently renovated by King Herod. The city and temple formed the natural backdrop for the climax of Jesus' ministry as he asserted his claim to be the nation's true prophet, priest and king. On his arrival, Jesus wept over the city, knowing that the so-called 'city of peace' did not know the things belonging to its peace' (Luke 19:41-44). Seven weeks later, during the annual summer feast of **Pentecost** the city was naturally full of Jewish pilgrims who had come up to worship in their mother-city.

Lord

This would become a key title for Jesus in the New Testament, and the earliest Christian **creed** was simply 'Jesus is Lord' (Rom. 10:9; 1 Cor. 12:3). Although the word *kurios* could mean simply a 'master' or 'boss', it had also served to translate the Hebraic references in the Old Testament to 'the Lord, the God of Israel'. So the apostles, in applying this title to Jesus so frequently, were evidently identifying Jesus in some way with Israel's God.

Messiah

This is a Hebrew term for 'the anointed person'. In biblical practice Israel's kings were 'anointed' with oil during their coronation, so the term refers to a royal figure. In the two centuries before Jesus Jewish hope for the arrival of this long-awaited royal king had steadily increased; and it was hoped he would liberate Israel from pagan domination. According to the Gospels Jesus himself made claims (both explicit and implicit) to be the Messiah – but not in all the senses that were expected. After the resurrection the apostles then assert that, despite some of these disturbed expectations, he was indeed the true Messiah. The Greek equivalent for Messiah is 'Christos'; so when the New Testament writers talk of 'Jesus Christ' they are effectively referring to 'King Jesus'.

Monotheism

'Monotheism' means belief in a single 'god', as opposed to 'polytheism' (belief in many 'gods'), atheism (belief in no 'god') or pantheism (belief that everything is 'god').

Nicene Creed, see Creed

Parousia, see Second Coming

Passover

Passover was one of Israel's three main festivals (along with Pentecost and Tabernacles). The festival celebrated how God, when bringing judgment on Egypt, had 'passed over' the Israelites' homes, sparing those houses which were marked by the blood of a lamb (as described in Exodus 12:1-36). Thereafter each year in the spring-time Jewish families would come together for a Passover meal. Jesus' Last Supper was essentially a Passover meal, but with some significant differences – there was probably no lamb on the table (pointing to Jesus being the true 'lamb') and it may well have been 24 hours ahead of the official schedule (since, by that time, Jesus would be dead). See further my book,

The Weekend that Changed the World (Marshall Pickering, 1999), pp. 4-5; and N.T. Wright, Jesus and the Victory of God (SPCK, 1996, p. 555-559).

Pentecost

This was Israel's second major religious festival, coming seven weeks or fifty days after **Passover** ('Pentecost comes from the Greek word for 'fifty'). It coincided with the barley harvest and was the time when Israel looked back to the giving of the Law at Mount Sinai (Exodus 20). Falling in mid-summer, the festival attracted a large number of international pilgrims from around the Mediterranean, and so was a fitting occasion for the dramatic outpouring of the Holy Spirit (described in Acts 2: p. 106).

Pharisees

These were religious Jews who belonged to one of the four main groups within the Judaism of Jesus' day (the others, according to Josephus, were the Sadducees, Essenes and Zealots). They were scattered throughout the land and believed God would vindicate Israel only when the 'people of the land' began to practise holiness and more fully obey God's commands. They also believed in the bodily resurrection of God's faithful people at the end of the age. The apostle Paul, before his conversion, had been an ardent Pharisee, with strong nationalistic tendencies.

Pontius Pilate

Pontius Pilate was the Roman governor (or 'procurator') in charge of the Roman province of Judea from AD 26 to AD 36. Though based most of the time in the provincial capital on the coast (Caesarea Maritima), he was naturally in Jerusalem during **Passover** – a season often marked by political unrest. Josephus (the Jewish historian writing c. 85 AD) indicates that he was particularly brutal and not afraid to provoke local opposition. His name was discovered in a Latin inscription found at Caesarea in 1961.

Samaritans

The Samaritans lived to the north of Jerusalem around the ancient city of Samaria. Their territory had been within the northern kingdom of Israel but its inhabitants had been taken into exile by the Assyrians in 722BC (the so-called 'ten lost tribes of Israel'). Those living there subsequently were viewed by the Jews as racially mixed and impure, and were remembered for their opposition to the rebuilding of the Jerusalem temple after the exile. Jesus shocked people with his positive attitude to the Samaritans (Luke 10:33; John 4:27).

So when the message about Jesus begins to reach Samaria (as described in Acts 8:4-17), this is a highly significant moment. Almost certainly, then, this is why the new believers in Samaria appear only to receive the Holy Spirit when the leading apostles arrive from Jerusalem – for this was a strategic moment, with the Spirit being received by the Jews' long-standing enemies. For both pastoral and 'political' reasons, this significant breakthrough needed to be witnessed and authorised by the apostles. This delay in receiving the Spirit is quite exceptional within the New Testament and so should not be taken as normative for today.

Satan, *see* **the Devil**

Second Coming

The Greek word often translated as 'Second Coming' is *parousia* (literally 'presence'). This word often described people being ushered into the presence of royalty. So, when the apostles speak of Jesus' *parousia*, they are focusing not so much on *how* Jesus will come again, but simply on the sure reality of his 'royal presence' at some point in the future (see Matt. 24:3f; 1 Cor. 15:23; 1 Thess 2:19; 3:13; 4:15; 5:23; 2 Thess. 2:1, 8-9; James 5:7-8; 1 John 2:28). Quite conceivably Jesus clarified this teaching about his *parousia* in the forty-day period after his resurrection (Acts 1:3): only now he had *come back from the dead*, could they understand his future *coming back from heaven*. Thereafter the apostles speak of this future hope on numerous occasions, warning both against cynicism about its delay or undue speculation as to its imminence (John 21:23; Col. 3:4; 2 Tim. 4: 1, 8; Heb. 10:25, 37; 1 John 1:3, 2 Pet. 3:4-10).

'Set' prayers

These are simply prayers that have been written down already (as opposed to spontaneous or 'free' prayer). They should not be dismissed as less 'spiritual' than other prayers – indeed many 'set' prayers, having been carefully prepared, prevent people from saying the wrong thing or wasting words (which Jesus warned against in Matt. 6:7). What matters in praying is not spontaneity, but sincerity.

Sinless perfection

Some 'holiness' movements within the church have suggested that 'sinless perfection' is possible in this life (basing their argument on texts such as 1 John 3:6 or Matt. 5:48). However, texts such as Rom. 7:23-24 clearly refer to the reality of on-going sin in believers' lives. The apostles' teaching thus combines a strong vision for holiness with a sober realism.

Son of God

This is one of the key terms used in the New Testament to describe Jesus. In the Old Testament it had been used to refer either to Israel or to her king, but now it comes to describe Jesus' unique relationship with God as Father: see e.g. Matt. 11:27; 16:16; Rom 1:4; John 1:14; see also **Christology**.

Speaking in tongues, *see* **Spiritual gifts**

Spiritual gifts

This translates a word used by Paul in 1 Corinthians (12:1), which simply means 'spiritual things'. However, Paul goes on to speak about the Spirit's *giving* of *charismata* ('gifts of grace'), so the concept of 'spiritual *gift*' is close to Paul's intention. Paul lists gifts such as 'wisdom' and 'prophecy'; he also includes 'speaking in tongues' (that is, praying with a special language other than your own mother-tongue), whilst urging people to use this (and every) gift with *agape* love. For other (clearly non-exhaustive) lists of such 'spiritual gifts', see also Eph. 4:11; Rom. 12:6-8, perhaps also 2 Pet. 1:4-7. These lists affirm that both seemingly 'supernatural' and 'natural' capacities may be given by the Holy Spirit.

Trinity

This is the doctrine that God has revealed himself in three persons as Father, Son and Holy Spirit. Although the word 'trinity' is not itself in the New Testament, there are good reasons for arguing that the New Testament writers were instinctively Trinitarian in the way they spoke of God: see further

Box 9c (p. 146–149).

NOTES